CW00858810

# Prospering in Spain

## The Escapades of a Mature Englishman and his Wife on the Spanish Coast

# Ken E. Tonks

# Introduction

When I told my wife Doreen one cool, clear autumn morning as we sat on our apartment balcony drinking coffee that I was thinking about writing a book, this is the response I got.

"You, Ken?" she asked with surprise.

"Why not?" I asked her back. "I've done some interesting things this year."

"That's true, but, well, I mean, you're not very… communicative, are you?"

"I speak when I've got something to say."

"Which is not very often," she said. "Not to me, at least."

"Well, we've been together so long that we read each other's thoughts," I said.

"I hadn't read that one, about the book."

"Ah," I replied, before heading to the bathroom. Once I'd made myself comfortable I thought some more about my statement about writing a book which, to be honest, had surprised me almost as much as her. Perhaps I'd had a meaningful but forgotten dream that night, but the truth is that I'd never thought about it before that morning. Doreen, you see, had already written a book about our move from England to Spain, but since we'd swapped our village house for an apartment down on the coast, her creative juices, such as they were, had dried up.

She put it down to having made plenty of friends here and being too busy to write much, whereas in the 'inhospitable' village she'd been so bored that she'd made notes every day, which she soon cobbled together into a book that, to my surprise, quite a few people have actually read.

Now I'm not the note-taking type, but we'd been in Spain for almost a year by that morning, mostly down on the coast, and with what passes for winter here setting in, I decided to act on my words. I'd had a curious little adventure, as you'll see, so I bought two large, lined notebooks, wrote for an hour or so every day for three months, and this is what I've come up with.

Doreen, who joined a local writing group where they seem to spend more time gabbing than writing, says that the result of my endeavours is, 'quirky, interesting, with elements of suspense, only occasionally offensive, but rather crudely expressed,' and has promised to 'tidy it up' and do whatever else needs doing to get it published, which is just as well, because me and computers don't get on.

Personally, when I've done a thing, it's done, so these few introductory words will be the last I write for a very long time. I've got better things to do now that spring is just around the corner.

# 1

I'd better start with a few words about how we ended up in Fuentecastillo, just along the coast from Malaga, because I can't expect everybody to have been lucky enough to have read my wife's short and rather biased book. Biased, I say, because she paints me as a grumpy, distant and sometimes even rude sort of bloke and herself as the heroine battling against adversity.

While I was out working at my friend Pedro's allotment or strenuously practising my Spanish in the bar, she, I think, was doing a bit too much moping around the house and spending hours glued to the computer, which I *know* cost a fortune to run with that dongle thing, even though she thinks I don't.

Now that we've got the internet she can spend as much time as she likes on it, which isn't so much now that she has friends and satellite telly, unlike in the village where the tight-fisted Shirley was the only person she ever knocked around with, and we could only get the Spanish channels.

Unbeknown to her, after the first month in the village I could see that she wasn't happy there, but I didn't let on as I wanted her to persevere and not throw in the towel straight away. People need a bit of 'tough love' sometimes and as I was so busy at the allotment and in the bar practising my

Spanish, that's what I gave her for a while. When it started to get colder, however, I saw that the village was no place for Doreen and if she hadn't begun to give me (what she thought were) subtle hints about moving to the coast, I would have started looking into it myself.

This is not reflected in her book, so I suppose that she didn't recognise the tough love that she was receiving or read the thoughts that I was having, and I can see that having a strong, silent type for a husband has its drawbacks when you're writing a book about the two of you. I hope that the reader will already be noticing that although it may be true that few words pass my lips, I do use them quite a lot in my head and am now trying my best to transfer them onto paper.

Doreen said that she hoped I would find writing cathartic, a word she must have learnt from one of her new friends – probably Janet, the retired schoolteacher – and I agreed that I might. When I looked the word up I saw what she, or Janet, meant, so perhaps writing this will release any hidden emotions that I've got, though I doubt it.

Anyway, after moving to the village from England in October, we ended up renting an apartment down here just before Christmas, having given the English landlords of the village house exactly zero notice of our departure, due to them having lied through their southern teeth to us about never having stayed there in winter, and leaving us with almost empty gas bottles.

My young friend Juan, a waiter from the village who has also moved down here now, told us that they took it just as badly as I'd hoped they would and that the bloke would like to have words with me. He's had a year to have them (the words) but hasn't approached me yet, probably fearing that I'm every inch the northern brute that my wife makes me out to be in her book. This is no longer true as I've mellowed a lot with age, sixty-six at the time of writing.

As soon as we got settled in here Doreen was so happy and busy that she couldn't think of anything else to write, so she brought her little book to a rather hurried close after having laid it aside for two months while she rediscovered her youth by meeting a lot of other middle-aged foreign women. I told her it was too short and that she should weave her burgeoning friendships into it (not in those exact words, but I didn't have her big thesaurus in front of me when I said it), but she wouldn't listen, being too busy with coffee mornings, exercise classes, bus trips, raising money for the animal sanctuary, and helping out in the charity shop; in short, all the things that middle-aged expat ladies do here.

Meanwhile, my own life followed quite a different course. True, I could also have sought out the expat contingent and whiled away the hours drinking beer or G&Ts and talking nonsense, but my superior Spanish meant that I could strike out into the community and talk, mostly nonsense, with the locals instead.

When we moved to Spain we both thought that Doreen would be the one to get to grips with the language first, as she'd spent a lot more time flicking through her phrasebook than me, after we had both given up on the baffling grammar book. My hours spent talking to Pedro at the allotment, and in the bar with him and the other blokes, paid off, and by the time we got to the coast I could understand just about everything that was said to me and make myself understood perfectly well without any of that grammar business.

Young Juan the waiter, who now works at a seafront restaurant here and shares a flat with his cousin, told me the other day that it was surprising how well I communicated in Spanish without needing to use many verbs, and I put this down to having got along with few verbs, or any other kind of words, in English for so many years. Doreen called me taciturn last week, but I think I'm just a good listener.

Before I tell you about my life here on the coast I'd better give you a short account of the two and a half months that we spent up in the village. This might be a useful lesson to those people who are thinking about coming to live in Spain and who wish to know how best to learn the language. While it may be true that years of studying is one way to go about it, I favoured the more direct approach, and still do.

On arriving in the village I asked myself where a good place to meet lots of local people would be, when they were in a relaxed frame of mind, and the only option I came up with was a local bar scruffy enough not to attract the *guiris*, which is what they call foreigners who they don't like here. After locating a suitable bar with Doreen one evening – our first, in fact – I soon realised that to further my Spanish studies I would have to go alone. Two foreigners together will never make any linguistic progress in a bar in Spain, especially, though I hate to say this, if one of them is a woman.

The rough and ready Spanish bar is still very much a male domain and to female readers I recommend the café terrace as a more suitable place for an exploratory chinwag, although the downside of this is that it's mostly foreigners who sit at the tables outside, or Spanish families and groups of friends who are not so open to informal approaches as the solitary, and preferably half-cut, local man.

Female linguists might have more luck frequenting the local shops, especially ones like the mercería (haberdashery) where an awful lot of chatting takes place over the purchase of a single button. Estancos (tobacconist's) are also a good bet and I keep urging Doreen to take up knitting or smoking in order to increase her exposure to the language.

So, on my second night in the village I toddled back to the bar, ordered a beer, and spoke to the bloke next to me. As luck would have it, that man was Pedro, who turned out to be our neighbour and soon became a firm friend of mine.

"Hola," I said.

"Hola," he replied.

"Yo, Ken," I said, pointing to myself.

"Yo soy Pedro," said Pedro.

"I am new here. Me and my wife have moved into a house just down the street," I said very slowly in English, accompanied by suitable gestures.

"You, street, there?" he asked, pointing.

"Sí," I said.

"Qué número?" he asked.

"What?" I asked.

"What number ... house?" he asked.

"Siete," I said, after a quick look in the phrasebook.

"Ah, yo vivo en el número nueve (9)," he said, which was the first sentence I'd ever understood in Spanish.

"Say it again," I said, twirling my finger horizontally, which means 'say it again' in every language.

"Yo vivo en el número nueve," he said, again.

"Yo," I said, before clearing my throat, "vivo en el número siete."

"Bien," he said, before slapping me on the back and buying me a beer.

There, in a nutshell, you have my method for learning Spanish. What you don't know, you say in English, with gestures, and if you don't understand their reply, you ask them to repeat it until you do, even if it means buying them a beer. If the bloke is not up for the challenge, you turn round and speak to the one on the other side. This is a method that can be employed just as successfully in the haberdashery or tobacconist's, I imagine, as there are always plenty of people hanging around, though the tongue-loosening effect of alcohol is often absent in those places.

Having suggested that my method is a simple one, I suppose I was quite lucky to bump into Pedro on my first solo outing, as he knew a bit of English and later introduced me to his mates. When Pedro was around, which was almost all the time, I could count on him to help me out when me or the bloke I was talking to got stuck, and after a month or so I could chat to them all even in his absence. I also employed this method on my first night in Fuentecastillo – by then needing hardly any English words to get the ball rolling – with similar success, but more about that later.

Pedro, as I've said, had an allotment and, after dropping some veg round on the following day, he soon invited me up to see it. I suppose I should describe Pedro, but he's just a bloke really, of about forty, normal height, short hair, fairly tanned, and always keen to be out and about.

The next Sunday we drove the mile or so up there in his car (which later belonged to me for a while), pulled up a few onions and carrots, and then sat down in the sun to drink a beer from the gas-powered fridge that he keeps in his little shed. We talked and mimed about sundry matters and picked a few weeds, before driving back to the bar for a bit of dinner, meaning lunch. We went back up there afterwards, had a nap on a couple of sunbeds that he fetched from the shed, picked another couple of weeds that must have sprung up while we were snoozing, drank another beer, and headed back to the bar.

After having been cooped up in a factory for the best part of fifty years, I saw straight away that the outdoor life suited me fine. I told Pedro this, so he gave me keys to the shed and an old moped and said I could go up to the allotment whenever I wanted. I got home a bit overtired after that first day and Doreen accused me of drinking too much, but after I'd been up a couple more times during the week and come back as sober as most judges, she changed her line of attack and said that he was exploiting me, which I often used to chuckle about as I sat up there in the sun sipping a beer and smoking my pipe.

Doreen was right about one thing in her book though, and I quote:

*'Ken, when the weather is nice, has a capacity for sitting in the sun with his pipe for hours on end, reading the paper, or just meditating, I suppose you'd call it, although he wouldn't.'*

Yes, my wife's right about that, though I certainly *would* call it meditating, but the pipe and slipper kind, not the sitting on a mat with your legs crossed variety, which doesn't look very comfortable at all.

So, to cut a short story even shorter, that was me sorted. Up to the allotment a few days a week, out to the bar a few evenings, and a bit of quality time with the wife; what more can a man ask for? Once we'd sorted our paperwork out with that gawky, money-grabbing, man-mad Swedish woman – 'Hella the Horrible' I used to call her, but Pedro always looked a bit sheepish when I mentioned her – and taken the hire car back to the airport, I could have stayed in the village for the rest of my life without being bored for a minute.

Things weren't so easy for poor Doreen, however, who was disappointed that her friendship with Shirley – a retired dental nurse with a Worzel Gummidge accent and our neighbour two doors up – turned out to be as tight as a duck's backside. After a couple of slightly annoying episodes, which Doreen greatly exaggerates in her book, she realised that she couldn't take her anywhere, without paying, so Shirley was put on the backburner, though she still turns up here now and again after some free grub and a moan about not being able to sell her house.

So, when I saw that the tough love experiment wasn't working, I let Doreen lure me down to the coast and take me on a meticulously planned tour of Fuentecastillo. I liked what I saw straight away and didn't need much persuading, so we rented an apartment at a very reasonable price – easily covered by the rent we get from our house in England – and moved in just before Christmas last year.

That, I see, is just about all I have to say about our life in the village, but one day at the allotment and one evening in the bar is much like another, so there's not much more to add, except that I still drive up to the allotment now and then and that all our acquaintances from the village either live here now (Juan), or want to sell up and move here (Hella and Shirley), or come down for the day every couple of weeks (Pedro). Our moving down here seems to have caused such a mobilisation that I tell Doreen that she must be a blooming magnet, though she's happy enough nowadays not to need much flattery.

# 2

Fuentecastillo is a biggish place with a nice promenade and a wide beach that is plenty long enough for my walks. When we moved into the fifth floor apartment I couldn't dismantle the bed in the little front bedroom fast enough and get a comfy armchair and a little table put in there instead. I've spent many a peaceful hour in that room, enjoying the partial sea views, and it's there that I'm writing this now. The rest of the flat is fine too, with furniture that Doreen likes and that I don't notice much, and the satellite TV keeps her happy when I'm out practising my Spanish.

On our first evening there Doreen was tired after the excitement of the move, so I decided to go for a stroll, taking my pipe and wallet just in case. After wandering down a couple of quiet streets I chanced upon a bar that looked all right – not too posh – so I went in to rest my legs.

In the time it took the waiter to pour my beer and shake some peanuts out of a big jar onto a little plate, I had overheard snippets of three conversations, none of them in Spanish. Three Scotchmen (I like calling Scotsmen Scotchmen) were talking in English, a youngish couple were jabbering away in French, and two blonde-haired, purple-faced blokes were talking some sort of Viking lingo. The waiter seemed to be the only native in the place, so I soon supped up and moved on.

When we first moved out here I imagined that I'd spend most of the little time I'd spend away from the wife with other British people and not have too much truck with the locals. I don't know why I thought like that really, just an ingrained loathing of all things foreign, I suppose, which was the way I was brought up. The only Spaniards I'd known had been the waiters and waitresses who had served us when we came here on holiday and I'd found them to be a surly bunch, on the whole.

On retrospect that doesn't surprise me as they were obviously overworked, probably underpaid, and had to put up with crowds of ignorant, beer-swilling foreigners all summer long. Seeing the way us lot splashed in the pool and splashed money about like there was no tomorrow, they were probably peeved about the hours they worked and the little they earned. I think they make a bit more and we spend a bit less nowadays.

So, assuming the locals would be like that, I hadn't expected to see eye to eye with them, but on that first night in the bar up in the village I saw that they weren't like that at all. They were all gabbing away, laughing, drinking beer, and watching the football. After the poncy foreigners I'd come across when we were looking at houses it came as a relief to see that they were regular blokes; just like me, in fact, except they talked a different language. I soon integrated into village life – or bar life, at least – and that was what I intended to do in Fuentecastillo.

I left that first bar and headed away from the sea, imagining that the locals would live in the normal flats on either side of the main road, rather than in apartments like ours. Sure enough, just before the main road I approached a bar where a lot of shouting was going on. Now, in England you might avoid a place like that, as the shouting would probably be leading up to a bout of fisticuffs – something I wasn't averse to in my younger days – but in Spain it's different. The more shouting that comes out of a bar, the better they're all getting on inside, so I went in and sat on a stool at the bar.

"Una caña, por favor," I said, because all the locals drink small beers or bottles here, a pint being considered a foreign aberration. Looking, as I do, a bit foreign myself, the waiter – who turned out to be the owner – seemed taken aback by the fluency of my speech, but as it was probably the sentence I'd practised most up to then, it came out just right. When I talk Spanish I don't slur my words, you see, like some foreigners, but say them snappy like they do.

"Quién juega?" I asked, pointing at the huge telly on the wall, even though I knew perfectly well that it was Malaga and Valencia.

"Málaga y Valencia," he said.

"Cómo van?" I asked, even though I could see that Valencia were winning 2-1.

"El Málaga va ganando dos-uno," he said.

"Muy bien," I said, Malaga being the local team. I'm not as big a football fan as I used to be, really, despite the amount of it I sat through up in the village bar, but they're serious about it here, especially if their team's playing, so if you show interest it's easier to become accepted as a regular bloke.

I ordered a few bits of octopus and a slab of dried blood, just to show that I wasn't squeamish, and I could see that he was a bit curious about me. I told him that I'd just moved into a flat in town and he asked me whereabouts it was. I said it was a couple of street that way, pointing towards the coast, as I didn't want him to know that I was renting a posh apartment. I told him that the wife and me had retired here and that I was keen to polish up my Spanish.

"Hablas bien," he said, meaning that I spoke well, which is a sad indictment on the other foreigners he must have met, because I was sure that I hadn't used many verbs, if any, but I'd got my message across.

He got a bit busy then, as it was half time, so I turned to a bloke who'd just come in and said hola. He asked me who was playing and who was winning, so I told him, before asking him if he was from the town. That sort of direct question might sometimes be taken the wrong way, but I don't think I'd pass for a gay bloke if I wore ballet tights, so he was happy to tell me that he was indeed a local man.

I'm terrible at describing people, especially blokes, as they always come out sounding the same, but I'll make an effort here because, just like with Pedro up in the village, I'd struck lucky with the first person, apart from the owner, who I'd spoken to. He was in his early fifties, about five foot seven, a bit tubby, with short greying hair and glasses. I bet you can picture him like he's standing in front of you! Doreen's been working on descriptions in her writing group, but if I ask her for help she'll try to do him from his fairly full head of stubbly hair right down to the tips of his toes, and after two pages of it you'd be none the wiser.

Federíco – Fede to his friends – told me that he worked as a bus driver, but what he really enjoyed doing was bricolaje, or DIY. I told him that I was quite keen on that too, which I used to be in England as it gave me something to do during the long winters, but that as I was renting a flat in town I couldn't do much now. He told me that he'd 'bricolajed' his own flat as much as his wife would let him and had now started on a little house he'd bought up in the hills.

This was something of a déjà vu moment, as it was my village friend Pedro's shack on his allotment that had led us to become such good friends. When blokes only have the house that they share with the missus, they're a bit like kids who have nowhere to play, so I decided to get myself into a talkative mood by ordering another beer, and one for him. I told him where we'd been living until recently and he said that he knew the village well and that it was a pity that it was getting overrun with guiris.

"I suppose I'm a guiri myself," I said.

"No, guiris don't come in here, and they don't speak Spanish as well as you do."

So that was twice I'd been complemented on my Spanish in the space of ten minutes, which made me think that real down to earth blokes didn't attach much importance to verbs, even though I was almost sure they used them whether they knew they did or not.

I seem to be mentioning verbs a lot, so I'd better explain why I've got a bee in my bonnet about them. It's not the verbs themselves – it's easy enough to learn the words for go, eat, drink, walk and so on – but what the Spanish do with them. The problem is that in every tense – and there are more of them than soft mick – there are *six* different endings. So, whereas we get along fine with 'I went, you went, he went' and so on, here you have to remember six different words to be able to say it properly.

Even if you make a special effort to remember all six ending for that tense, it doesn't get you very far as you have to do the same for all the other tenses, like present, future and a few more that I can't see much use in. Multiply all that effort by about a million verbs and you can see why I gave up on the damn things on about my second day in Spain.

It was a great relief not to have to bother thinking about them and I found that it freed up a lot of grey matter for learning all the normal, useful words that you need to have a conversation. One final point before you start thinking that I'm obsessed by grammar: when I say I don't use verbs, I mean that I don't bother *conjugating* them, which is the fancy word for using all the right endings. If I want to say eat, drink, smoke or walk, I just say comer, beber, fumar or andar and stick on a word like yesterday, today or tomorrow to explain when whatever I'm talking about is happening. If you follow my advice you'll be as fluent as I am in no time, and not be umming and ahhing for ten minutes just to say something like, 'I ate fish,' which is what Doreen still does.

Anyway, me and Fede got on like a house on fire that first evening and at about half eleven we both decided that we'd better get back to the wives. He didn't invite me to see his house up in the hills, but I knew he would sooner or later and I hoped it would be a bit nearer than Pedro's shack on his bit of land which now takes over half an hour to get to, even if you don't get stuck behind a tractor.

The first few days in Fuentecastillo were a bit tiresome, as Doreen insisted on us going out exploring together and having umpteen meals, coffees and beers in lots of different places. It wasn't the expense that bothered me, because with the rent from our house in England and our pensions we had plenty of cash, but Doreen was so excited about being there that she talked nineteen to the dozen all day long.

It was a relief when we found the café where a lot of British women spend most mornings and some afternoons nattering. She knew straight away that it was the place for her and the next morning she headed off there on her own like an intrepid explorer.

She soon got to know Janet, the retired teacher from Woking, Barbara, the retired hairdresser from Carlisle, and Mildred, the retired housewife from Devon, as well as a few more British and Irish women. I don't see them often myself, but I feel like I've know them all my life by now. Doreen says that whatever she says to me goes in one ear and comes out of the other, but it must not do because if you gave me a quiz on Janet, Barbara and Mildred's grandchildren I'd probably do quite well.

So, once my wife started having a social life again – she can tell you all about that if her writing group assignments ever leave her with enough time to write anything worthwhile – I was free to go my own way. Although it was the middle of winter, it was like being on a different planet from up in the village, and rather than sitting with my coat and hat on up at Pedro's allotment, I was strolling down the beach with my cardigan over my shoulder and my trousers rolled up.

My balding head was soon as brown as a berry and I got to know most of the waiters in the seafront cafes where I'd go for a refreshing beer or the occasional coffee. After dinner at home and an update from Doreen on her flourishing friendships, I'd toddle down to the bar to have a chat with Fede and some of the other blokes who I was getting to know.

That was the life, but after about a week I felt the tug of the mountains and decided to drive up to the village to spend the day at Pedro's allotment. I chose an especially fine day, of course, and phoned Pedro to say that I was going, so after spending the morning at the allotment, where I picked a few weeds and enjoyed the fine view, I met him at the bar for dinner, meaning lunch. (I'll just call dinner lunch from now on, I think, like Doreen's started to do.)

They were all pleased to see me there, said I was looking well, and asked if I'd become a guiri now that I was down on the coast. I was able to tell them proudly that I hadn't made a single foreign friend and that I'd found a bar almost, but not quite, as good as theirs.

"I'll come down one Sunday and we'll go fishing," Pedro said when we'd sat down to eat.

"You do that. I'll buy you lunch afterwards," I said, in my own way.

We talked about this and that, but men aren't like women, who have to tell each other everything that's happened since they last sat down together to tell each other about everything that had happened since the time before that. Nothing much had changed in the village, although it had only been a few weeks since I'd been living there, and though I liked Pedro and his allotment as much as ever, I knew that my future lay down on the coast. As I drove down the windy road that used to drive Doreen mad, I thought about how picturesque it was up in the mountains, but reflected that I could see them from down on the coast too, where it was a lot warmer and better for walking.

So, being a fairly easy man to please, I soon got into my new routine which I liked even more than my old one, with the added bonus that Doreen was much happier than she had been in the village and didn't nag me about not spending any time at home, mainly because she wasn't there too often either. As far as I was concerned, my life could have gone on like that indefinitely, or at least until I snuffed it, but that wouldn't make much of a book. No, I'm writing this mostly because of the unusual things that started to happen once I got to know my new pal Fede a little better.

# 3

After the tiresome Christmas and New Year celebrations that Doreen forced me to go along to with her new friends and their solidly expat husbands – all with their bodies in Spain but their minds back in Britain – I got into a nice routine of going to my new local bar a few times a week, usually on the same evenings that Fede's wife let him out.

We were getting on so well, Fede and me, that if it was too busy up at the bar we sometimes sat down at a table to be able to chat more privately and not have blokes asking us the football score every five minutes. It seemed a bit effeminate to me at first – going to sit at a table – but I soon got used to it. I am a pensioner, after all, and standing up all the time reminded me of the factory, which I was still doing my best to forget after nearly fifty years of it.

Anyway, it struck me after a few meetings that despite us having so much to talk about, he still hadn't invited me to go up to see his little house in the country. He was taking so long about it, in fact, that I'd started to wonder if there was some reason why he was dragging his feet so much.

Perhaps he had a bit on the side who he met up there, I thought, though I doubted it as he didn't seem especially interested in the opposite sex. Like me he was happy for his missus to make her own fun, which I think she did in much the same way as Doreen – nattering with her friends – though she also had two small grandchildren in town who took up quite a bit of her time.

It was one Thursday night towards the end of January when I decided to drop a few hints to Fede about him inviting me to his house in the hills.

"Are you working at all this weekend, Fede?" I asked, because, being a bus driver, he sometimes had to do the odd Saturday or Sunday.

"No, Ken, I'll be home tomorrow at six."

"Up to the house on Saturday then, I suppose?" I asked.

"Yes, lots to do up there."

"Ah," I said, trying to inject a lot of curiosity into the word. "Another beer?"

"Go on then, Ken. One more won't hurt."

I'd better point out right away that when I translate my conversations with Fede, or anyone else, I'm not suggesting that my Spanish was so correct, but if I tried to translate it word for word it would make very tiresome reading. The main thing is that he understood me perfectly well and never bothered correcting my little mistakes and omissions, which was fine by me, as he'd only have confused me.

I brought two more bottles of beer back from the bar and decided to pursue the subject of the house in the hills until he either invited me there or told me why he wouldn't or couldn't ask me along.

"What do you get up to in the country, Fede?"

"Oh, DIY mostly."

"What are you working on at the moment?" I asked, not feeling averse to giving him a hand if he asked me to.

"I'm, er…" he began, before peering at me through his oval specs, "doing this and that."

"Building?" I asked.

"Not now, no."

"Plumbing?"

"No."

"Woodwork? Electrics? Painting? Gardening?" I asked, throwing subtlety to the wind. I've always called a spade a spade and Fede always called a pala a pala too, except where his country place was concerned.

One of these last things made an impact on him, because he took off his glasses and polished them on a paper napkin, before putting them slowly back on. I only wear glasses for reading, but I also know how to use them to buy time if Doreen's nagging me about something, which she wasn't doing very often by that time, being so busy. I sipped my beer and waited.

"The fact is, Ken, that I'm working on a project up there."

"Right. What sort of project?"

"Well, it's a bit secret."

"Ah."

"That's why I haven't invited you up there."

"Right."

"The wife doesn't go either, or anybody else."

If he thought that this would make me feel better he was right, because I was a new friend, after all, and as no-one else was allowed up there I didn't feel as miffed as I'd been starting to feel about not getting an invite.

"Right, I understand," I said. "A bit of rain tomorrow, they say."

"Yes, in the morning."

"Fining up in the afternoon."

"Yes."

"And staying fine all weekend," I said, bringing the subject skilfully back round to his free time. "I'm just nipping out for a quick smoke."

When I returned from my rather long smoke I could see that Fede was dying to spill the beans. He was sort of fidgety and couldn't leave his glasses alone, so I decided to bide my time. He finally leant over the table and spoke, almost in a whisper.

"I don't want anyone to know what I'm up to yet," he said.

"Vale," I said, meaning 'right'.

"Because... well, I'm not really sure if what I'm doing is on the right lines or not."

"Vale." I looked at my watch. "It's about time I got going," I said, supping up.

"You wouldn't tell anyone, would you, Ken?"

"What?"

"About my project?"

"Oh, that. No, of course not."

"Not even your wife?"

"Least of all her."

"Well," he said, his brown eyes sparkling a bit. "If you want I'll pick you up here at about nine on Saturday morning and you can come and see for yourself."

"Great, Fede. I'm intrigued."

"We'll spend the day up there."

"Great."

"But not a word to a soul," he said, tapping his nose so that anyone looking our way would know that he had just told me something confidential.

He seemed more relaxed after that, having got his big secret off his mind, or at least the fact that he had one, which was a start. As I wandered homeward I couldn't help wondering what sort of thing he was up to, and as I lay in bed that night listening to Doreen's light snoring I started to make a mental list of the things it might be.

By the time I went for my pre-lunch stroll the next day – a sunny but slightly chilly one – I'd narrowed it down to three main possibilities. It might be something mechanical, as he'd told me that he always fettled his own cars, so I thought he might be doing up some kind of vehicle. It could also be something to do with carpentry, because I knew that he'd built his own shed some time ago, so maybe it was some type of wooden contraption. My third guess was a gardening project, as he'd implied that he was quite green-fingered, so perhaps he was growing something special, like huge sunflowers, melons or whatever.

"I'm off to my friend Fede's for the day tomorrow," I told Doreen that evening, having given the bar a miss, just for a change.

"Oh, I thought we were going to have lunch at the restaurant where Juan works," she said after the EastEnders theme tune had finally faded away.

"Were we? Well, we can go on Sunday instead."

"I thought Pedro was coming down from the village on Sunday."

"That's true. Well, if he comes down alone he can come along and I'll pay. If he brings the family he can choose where to eat, because I'm not paying for all four of them."

"That's just like you, Ken," she said with a fond smile.

"Too right. Anyway, I think he'll know to come alone as the whole point is for us to have a quiet morning's fishing."

"And then have lunch with me."

"Of course, dear," I said, because I know how to turn on the charm as well as the next man. "Unless he brings butties."

"Oh, Ken!"

"I'll ring him and tell him not to."

"Good. I hope you don't come back drunk from this Fede's house tomorrow, like you did the first time you went to Pedro's allotment," she said, just for form's sake, really, as she wasn't using her nagging voice.

"No, Fede's not much of a drinker, and nor am I nowadays," I said, which wasn't untrue as I rarely polished off more than five bottles or seven cañas in a session any more, and hardly ever drank in the flat.

"I'd like to meet him sometime, you know, so I know who you're going around with," Doreen said. "I mean, I introduced you to Janet, Mildred, Barbara and their husbands."

"Not Barbara's you didn't."

"That's because he's dead, dear."

"Janet and Mildred's blokes will be following him soon if they keep knocking back the wine, G&Ts and whiskies like they do."

"I think Harvey and Geoffrey are quite refined," she said.

"Refined? Because they drive posh cars? They wouldn't know a book if it hit them on the back of the head."

"You don't read that much, Ken, and you drink too."

"Look at my nose. What do you see?"

"Well, a biggish nose."

"What colour is it?"

"Quite brown now, I suppose."

"Whereas Harvey's looks like a rotting raspberry, and Geoffrey's cheeks look like a roadmap with all those veins. Spirits are too strong here to sup them like they do. It's because they're bored, of course."

"You don't exactly do a lot of exciting things, Ken."

"That might all change tomorrow."

"Why's that?"

"I don't know, but I've just got a feeling that Fede's up to something very interesting at his little house in the hills."

"Like what?"

"I don't know. He hasn't told me yet. I'll be the first person to find out. Even his wife doesn't seem to know."

"What do you think it might be?" she asked, all ears.

"I don't know, but don't get too excited about it as I shan't be able to tell you."

"Oh, Ken! I'm your wife."

"And a blabbermouth."

"Not true," she said, giving me a friendly shove, as I was sitting on the settee for once.

"Anyway, all will be revealed tomorrow... to me."

"Ha, I'll worm it out of you," she said, putting her hand on the back of my neck and giving it a squeeze.

I knew what those squeezes meant and, not being in one of my rare amorous moods, I got myself off to bed and put my sleeping mask on double quick.

# 4

The next morning, after coffees with a splash of brandy to warm us up, we climbed into Fede's little car and trundled off down the coast road. When he turned left and drove under the motorway I could see we were heading towards the village where me and Doreen used to live, and I hoped we wouldn't be going too far up that extremely twisting road. After three or four miles I could see a biggish village up ahead, before which, to my relief, he turned left onto a country lane that took us past a couple of the huge plastic greenhouses that litter the countryside around there.

After a few minutes he turned off onto a track and pulled up outside a little white bungalow set in the middle of a small plot of land. Fede hadn't said much since we'd met and seemed to get a bit tense as we approached the house. I hoped he wasn't going to show me a load of dead bodies that he was busy stuffing or pickling, but he didn't seem the type to go in for that sort of thing.

As we walked towards the house I suspected that his surprise wasn't going to be a horticultural one, as most of his land seemed to be lying fallow, apart from a few spuds and onions that I spotted. As he reached towards the door with his key he seemed to have second thoughts.

"Er, Ken, do you mind sitting down over there on one of those plastic chairs for a minute while I sort a few things out inside?"

"No problem, Fede. I'm ready for a smoke anyway," I said, pulling my pipe from my jacket pocket and wiping the dust off one of the white chairs.

As I puffed away I could hear him pulling up all the blinds, after which I heard a few shuffling and scraping sounds. I was certainly intrigued when he finally reappeared and beckoned me towards the door.

"I'm going to wait out here while you take a look, Ken. There's plenty of light, so just take your time and look round all the rooms, though there isn't much to see in the kitchen or bathroom."

"Vale," I said, feeling a great sense of anticipation. I walked straight through to the largish living room and imagine my surprise when I found myself surrounded by paintings. And I mean surrounded, because as well as several pictures on easels, there were lots more hanging and leaning on the walls, and even the walls themselves had been given a good seeing to by Fede's brushes.

There were more pictures in the two bedrooms, mostly leaning against the walls, and a few stacked up in the kitchen, though I guessed they were the ones that he hadn't chosen for his impromptu display. I thought Fede would come inside to see what I thought, but he didn't, so, guessing that he wanted my considered opinion, I walked round again and tried to form one.

As you can probably imagine, I'm no art connoisseur, but I'll try to describe Fede's style for you. It was modern, that's for sure, and pretty abstract, but not so abstract that you couldn't see that each picture was supposed to represent something. He used vivid colours and seemed quite keen on getting a sort of swirling effect, but I could see that he wasn't one of these modern artists who can't paint for toffee.

I mean, there were quite a few sketches lying around too, which looked just like whatever it was that he was drawing, and you could see that he was very skilful. To give you an example, there was one sketch of an old woman sat on a chair in a doorway. He'd done the wrinkles on her face brilliantly and made her hands very lifelike, and even I knew that hands were especially hard to draw. Near the sketch there was a painting – in oils, I thought, correctly – done from the sketch, and it was here that he'd got carried away with all his swirls and strange colours until you could hardly see that it was an old woman at all.

As well as quite a few portraits like that, he'd also done a lot of pictures of village scenes, landscapes and a few seascapes. Some of them were pretty overpowering, what with the gaudy, swirling colours, and I can't say that I'd have liked to have had most of them in my living room, apart from the sketches, which were more my cup of tea.

"What do you think, then?" asked Fede, having crept in while I was examining a big canvas of a mountain that looked a bit like an erupting volcano, but clearly wasn't.

"You're very talented," I said, because there was no denying that. "When did you learn to draw and paint like this?"

"Oh, I've been at it all my life, on and off, but for the last three years I've spent most of my free weekends up here," he said, seeming relieved that I hadn't said, 'What the hell is *that* supposed to be?' or anything like that.

"So does your wife not know what you're up to?" I asked, because I imagined that she'd be a bit peeved about having her country place turned into an artist's studio.

"Oh, she knows, but she doesn't like coming up here much in winter anyway."

"What about in summer?" I asked, imagining what Doreen would think about living in a house packed to the rafters with pictures and art paraphernalia.

"She's given me an ultimatum," he said, looking glum.

"What kind of an ultimatum, Fede?"

"Well, she's not against me painting, within reason, because she knows I'm good, but she wants me to start getting rid of pictures and to just use the spare room as a studio. I have to repaint all the walls before summer too, white."

"That sounds fair enough. I mean, the spare room's got good light and if you keep on painting more and more you won't be able to move at all."

"She wants me to start selling them," he said, gazing around the living room cum studio.

"Sounds reasonable. I think that's what most artists do."

"I've never tried to sell one."

"Never?"

"Never. Oh, I've given a few away to relatives, but... well, I wouldn't really know how to go about selling them, and I'm not sure if anybody would want them. They're a bit experimental, you see."

"Isn't most modern art experimental?" I asked.

"I guess so, but I'm not sure how mine will be received. I'm afraid that people won't understand them, or they'll think they're as bad as some of the rubbish you see in the shops and galleries in Málaga."

"Is that all rubbish, then?"

"No, not all of it. That's the trouble with modern art, you see. Some artists are incredibly talented and others are impostors, but it's who you know as much as what you know in that little world. What do you think of Picasso, Ken?"

This wasn't a question I felt very well qualified to answer, but I had let Doreen drag me round his museum in Malaga, so I'd seen a fair amount of his work. I decided that honesty was the best policy.

"I think he was a bit daft," I said.

"Go on."

"Well, he was brilliant, wasn't he? I mean, some of the stuff he did when he was about fifteen showed that he could have been a great master."

"*Could* have been?" he asked, poker-faced.

"Yes, he could have painted as well as Michelangelo or... any of them," I said, finding my mind suddenly empty of any more great masters.

"I agree, but all that had been done before."

"He could have just done more of it."

"Hmm, yes, but art has to move forward," he said.

"Why?"

Fede laughed, stumped by my challenging question.

When I later took a look at a couple of art books that he lent me, it seemed to me that it was the Impressionists who had first started to lose the plot, after which Van Gogh and the other Post-Impressionists started painting even more weird stuff. When I got onto the first Symbolist and Abstract painters, I lost interest and went back to look at the proper artists again. The books just confirmed my opinions, really, but let's get back to that morning at Fede's.

"Anyway," he said. "Now I'm going to have to try to sell some, whether I like it or not."

"Hmm," I said, surveying the room and putting my thinking cap on.

I think it was at that moment when I had a bit of an epiphany, if that's the word. My mind sort of perceived a host of new horizons opening up before me, though I couldn't quite put my finger on any of them. As I said, I was quite content to potter on as I had been doing, and I had a great ability for not getting vexed or bored, especially if the sun was shining and I knew that Doreen was keeping herself entertained. Having said that, I wasn't averse to experiencing new things, especially if I'd be experiencing them in the company of someone I got on with, like Fede.

"I'll help you to sell some paintings," I found myself saying.

"*You*, Ken?" he asked, in a tone slightly reminiscent of my dear wife.

"Why not? If I set my mind to something, I can always do it," I said, the secret to this true statement being that as I'd set myself relatively few challenges during my uneventful life, I'd managed to achieve them all. Here's a list of most of them:

Win the Sunday School Sponsored Silence – done.
Get a job in a factory at sixteen – done.
Get and stay married – done.
Have two children – done.
Leave the factory at sixty-five – done.
Move to Spain – done.

So, with my 100% record of achievement I didn't see why I couldn't help Fede to sell his paintings if I put my mind to it.

"All this secrecy will have to end, of course," I said.

"I guess so, but I have to be sure that my art is valid, Ken," he said, polishing his glasses for the umpteenth time.

"It is. You can take my word for it."

"Thanks, Ken, but… well, you're not really an art expert, are you?"

"Is that who you're going to sell to? So-called art experts?"

"Well, no."

"Exactly. You're going to sell to…" I searched my mind for the Spanish word for 'punters', but couldn't think of it. "You're going to sell to normal people, aren't you?"

"I suppose so."

"Well, people don't get much more normal than me and I'm telling you that your paintings are good."

"Do you *like* them, though?"

"Not really, no, apart from the drawings and a few of the landscapes, but that's not the point."

"Isn't it?"

"No, the truth is that I'll a bit *too* normal to be your typical picture buyer. I mean, I know that Doreen's put some stuff up on the walls of the flat, but I can't say I've noticed what they are. No, I'm not a great consumer of art, but I bet I know a lot of people who are."

"Who?"

"The guiris, Fede, the guiris. Who else?"

"Hmm, I don't know many guiris… I mean foreigners."

"Don't mind saying guiri to me, Fede."

"I mean, I see them all the time on the buses, but the only foreigner I actually know is you."

"And through me, my friend, you can reach hundreds of the buggers. Is there any beer in the fridge?"

"Yes."

"Let's go and sit in the sun and drink a couple."

# 5

We hardly entered the house again during the rest of the day. After a couple of beers and a good smoke – me, not Fede, as he had quit – we drove up into the village by another lane to get some lunch.

"I feel a bit guilty about not painting today," he said with a nervous laugh as we pulled up outside a scruffy bar.

"No, today is a day for reflection and looking ahead, Fede."

"I suppose so."

"And we're going to be busy at the weekends from now on."

"Are we?"

"Oh, yes," I said, with a confidence that wasn't quite warranted, but I wanted to clear my friend's mind of self-doubt. "I'll need to tell my wife about it. She's the one who knows all the guiris, being one herself."

"Vale."

"She's friendly with a few, who are friendly with a few more, and so on."

"English people?"

"Mainly British, yes, but I think most of the others will speak English too, apart from the French, and I can't see them spending money on paintings anyway."

"Why not?"

On him asking me this I realised that my very slight and almost always latent racism had reared its ugly head for a moment, so I told him we'd soon get the nice French people coughing up the euros too.

"I only speak Spanish, Ken."

"That's a good thing."

"Why?"

"Because you won't be able to answer any of their stupid questions. You'll be the mysterious artist and I'll be your taciturn assistant," I said. "We'll be... impenetrable."

"Will that be a good thing, Ken?"

"Yes, I mean, do you *want* to explain your paintings?"

"I don't think I could."

"There you are then. Let's order some food."

After a hearty meal and a couple of bottles of cheap but palatable red wine I took the wheel, as we couldn't risk Fede losing his bus driver's licence. After soaking up the mild winter sun for a while longer I finally allowed Fede back into the house. He looked longingly at his palette and brushes, but I turned his attention to his existing works.

"When we go off selling we'll take my car, as it's bigger than yours and with the back seats down we'll get a lot of pictures in it," I said. "We need to choose about twenty that you want to sell."

"Right, and some sketches?"

"No, no sketches yet."

"Why not?"

"Well, they're good, but they take away the mystery."

"Do they?"

"Yes, they show how you arrived at your wonderful creations," I said, feeling quite expansive after our lunchtime tipple. "We want to keep them guessing."

"Do we?"

"Yes, it's all about the mystery. It'll be a mystery to them why they like them and a mystery why they've ended up parting with a couple of hundred euros for one, ha ha."

"That sounds a bit cynical, Ken."

"Maybe, but I'm the commercial brains behind this, so leave that to me," I said, and as I spoke I marvelled at what I was saying. There was no way that I could have said anything like that in English, but in (very bad) Spanish it somehow seemed all right; a bit like playacting, which I suppose it was really. I mean, I'd never had much fun in the factory, apart from a few practical jokes, so it was about time I let my hair down a bit, despite not having much actual hair left.

Fede walked around the room, fingering the odd canvas, before shaking his head and turning to face me.

"I think you'd better choose them, Ken."

"Why's that?"

"Well, it's hard for me to be objective."

"Are there any you don't want to sell?"

"A few."

"Right, take those into the spare room and bring the ones in there in here."

After faffing around for a bit he selected four canvases and took them to the spare room. I was quite pleased with his choices as they were among the weirdest ones. You could hardly tell what they were supposed to be and I thought the punters would quite like to have an inkling about if it was a person, building, mountain or sea view that they were spending good money on.

While I was choosing I tried to put myself into the shoes of a potential buyer. None of the paintings were going to be cheap, not at first anyway, and if I was going to spend a three-figure sum on an artwork I'd want it to be fairly big, look like it had taken a long time to do, and I'd want to be able to tell what it was. After choosing about a dozen in this way I realised that they'd take up a lot of space on whichever walls they were going to be displayed, so I chose a few smaller ones too, in case we came across any poor but discerning guiris on our travels.

Travel, you see, was something that I planned us to do quite a bit of, as I had no intention of standing around in Fuentecastillo hawking paintings. Besides, they say that no man is a prophet in his own land and, if this proved to be true in Fede's case, I planned to take our travelling art show at least as far as the foreigner-infested villages up in the mountains, if not further.

"What do you think of my choices, Fede?" I asked when I'd come out of my reverie.

"Quite good, Ken, but I think you've missed some of my best ones."

"Like what?"

"Well, this church tower here and that group of children there," he said.

"Which is which?"

"Here are the children," he said, pointing to some splodges.

"Right, well, if you think they're your best, that's good, because you'll be able to get big money for them once you're famous."

"You don't really think I'll become famous, do you?" he asked, his plump, rather naïve face breaking into a worried smile.

"Not famous, no, but maybe a bit better known," I said, wanting to keep his feet on the ground.

"I'd *love* to be able to give up driving buses, Ken."

"Would you? I'd have thought it was quite a nice job."

"Oh, I like being out on the open road, but it's driving into all the bus stations I don't like, and hanging around with the other drivers. I'm not like them anymore."

"What do you mean?"

"Well, since I took up art seriously I find their talk a bit boring. It's all football and griping about the company we work for. I sit there wishing I was up here painting."

"It's funny that you and me have become friends, then, because I'm not exactly the artistic type, am I?"

"Oh, I don't want to talk about art, but with you I talk about different things than I would with the people in town, and I find that refreshing."

"Right," I said, not wanting him to bare his soul to me there and then. Spanish blokes are a bit like that though, once you get to know them. They're more direct and sincere than English blokes, who have to get hammered before they'll open up, and some, like me, not even then.

"Do you think we should frame them, Ken?"

"Hmm, I don't know. I think they look good as they are on their wooden frames, though we'll have to protect them.

They're less bulky that way too. Ah, I see you haven't signed them."

"No, not yet. This old one over here's signed," he said, extracting a small painting from the pile in the kitchen. "This is one of my earlier efforts."

It was an oil painting of an old fishing boat that looked remarkably like an old fishing boat, with 'Federico Pérez Martín' painted in small, clear letters in the bottom right-hand corner. As I examined the picture Fede began to titter.

"It's terrible, isn't it? So basic. I'd throw it out, but I keep it to show myself how far I've progressed."

"I like it better than most of the others," I said, but on seeing his crestfallen look I added, "but that's because I'm ignorant about art."

"If you like it you can keep it."

"Oh, thanks, Fede. I'll get it framed next week and put it up. I like your nice clear signature too, but it won't do."

"No?"

"No. Federico's all right, because that poet chap Lorca was called that, I think, but your surnames are just too common."

"Do you think I should change my name? I don't think my wife would like that."

"No, but…" I thought deeply for a while. "I know. We'll just use your initials. It'll add to the mystery, but you'll have to make them look interesting."

This gave Fede the excuse he'd been looking for to mix some paint and after a few tries on a bit of old canvas he came up with an 'F.P.M' that was just the ticket; sort of tremulous and, well, mysterious.

"Shall I put it on your painting, Ken?"

"No, I want mine to be by the old Fede, before you became a well-known artist."

"You can be my manager," he said, which just showed how contagious my ill-informed enthusiasm had proven to be.

"I've got plenty of money, Fede. I'll just help you out and we'll have some fun."

"Well, if I do sell some you're certainly going to get a share," he said quite sternly, for him.

"We'll see," I said, because if Fede was going to start coining it in, I certainly wasn't averse to having a few spare doubloons tossed my way.

"That's a nice little picture," said Doreen when I arrived home a while later.

"It's one of Fede's," I said, leaning it against the toaster.

"Your friend? I didn't know he was an artist," she said, looking quite pleased by the idea. "Was that his big secret?"

"Yes, but not anymore. He's very talented," I said, having hatched a plan on my walk back from the bar to the flat.

"You never mentioned his painting before."

"Well, he's a bit shy about it. One of these hidden geniuses, you know."

"Hmm, well, that picture of the fishing boat's very well done, but I don't know if it makes him a genius," she said, so intrigued that she hadn't even moaned about me lighting my pipe in the flat.

"He painted that when he was about fourteen," I lied. "What he does now is a lot more experimental and abstract. I think it's about time the world found out about him," I said, very sombrely, despite the three beers that I'd just knocked back with Fede to celebrate his future success.

"So did you really not know he was a painter, Ken?"

"Oh, I've *known* since about the second time I spoke to him, but today's the first time I've seen the pictures. He's decided I'm someone he can confide in."

"You, Ken?"

"Why not? He could tell I wasn't the blabbing type and he had to tell someone."

"Didn't you say he had a wife and kids?"

"Yes, but the kids have flown the nest. His wife... well, she's not very cultured and doesn't really understand why he does it."

"I'd *love* it if you took up painting, Ken," she said, pawing at my arm.

"I can't see that happening, but I'm going to help Fede to sell his pictures."

"You, Ken?"

"Yes, *me*, Doreen."

"And how are you going to do that?"

"I'm still working out the finer details."

"I could tell Janet, Mildred, Barbara and the others."

"Yes, but don't tell them just yet. I'm still trying to decide what our... approach will be."

"It all sounds very mysterious," she said, following me round the settee to try to paw me again.

"It's all about the mystery," I said softly, before switching on the telly.

# 6

Fishing is quite a good activity for getting the old grey matter moving, so the next morning, once I'd exchanged a few pleasantries with Pedro and we'd set up the two rods he'd brought down from the village, I settled down to consider how best to help Fede sell his paintings.

As he was often in Malaga, he'd agreed to buy plenty of plastic bags and bubble wrap to keep the pictures safe and clean, so all we had to do was load them into my car and set off. But where to? I knew that the obvious thing to do was to tout the pictures round the art shops and galleries in the city, but I had a feeling that this wouldn't get us very far. I didn't like cities anyway and I thought that the expats would be more likely to buy pictures in the quaint little villages or the smaller seaside places, where they'd be more relaxed and not distracted by churches, museums, posh shops, and so on.

Then there was our image to consider. I mean, Fede's a nondescript, tubby little chap and I'm a big, stoutish, foreign-looking bloke, so if we just hauled the paintings out at a market or something the punters would probably think they'd been done by someone else, or even that we'd stolen them. I didn't fancy dressing up myself, but I thought that Fede ought to look the part a bit more than he did. I'd just decided to consult Doreen about that when I saw that Pedro was reeling in.

"Anything?" I asked.

"No, I'm just checking the bait." He swung the weighted line towards him and inspected the nasty-looking worms that he'd bought that morning. "Not even a nibble," he said, unperturbed, before casting out again.

"Pedro, if someone wanted to sell some pictures up in the village, what would be the best way to go about it."

"What sort of pictures?"

"Painted pictures. Sort of abstract, but very good."

"I'm not really the man to ask, but... I don't know, maybe at the market on Saturday. Or try to get one of the restaurants to put a few up. Who's the painter? You?"

"Ha, not me, no. He's a friend of mine here in town called Fede. Bus driver by day, artistic genius by night," I said, because it sounded good, and he did get out to the house to paint some evenings.

"What are the paintings like?" he asked.

"Well, they're..." I began. As I was thinking, another idea occurred to me, to add to the one Pedro had just given me about the restaurants. "They're hard to describe, but we're going to get a catalogue printed," I said, because that's how fast my old brain was working just then.

"We?"

"I'm going to be his commercial agent."

"You, Ken?"

"Yes, me, Pedro."

"Right," he said doubtfully.

"I know an unknown genius when I see one and we're both going to make a lot of money," I said.

I could have been completely sincere with Pedro, as he was a good friend, but if I was going to be doing a lot of bullshitting, if you'll pardon the expression, I thought I might as well start as I meant to go on. Besides, I hadn't written off the natives as potential buyers and Pedro would spread the word in his local bar and beyond if I asked him to.

"Well, you might as well give it a go, Ken. You've got plenty of time, after all."

"Exactly," I said, pleased by his encouraging words. "That's a good idea about the restaurants. Do you think any of the ones in the village would be interested? They'd get a commission, of course, and so would you if you got them to take a few paintings."

"I'm sure Pepe at the bar would put up one or two if I asked."

"Hmm, thanks, but I'm thinking about the guiris, really. Most of the pictures will cost at least two hundred euros."

"That's a lot."

"As I say, the man's a genius and, well, we all want to make a bit of money, don't we?" I said, giving him a mischievous, greedy sort of look.

It's horses for courses, you see, and while I wouldn't have dreamt of speaking like that to an arty-farty type, I knew that Pedro was as fond of cash as the next man.

"I'll ask around. Better still, give me a few catalogues when they're ready and I'll call in with those."

"Thanks, Pedro, I will."

"How much will I get?"

"Ten percent of the sale price," I said, off the top of my head.

"And how much for you?" he asked with a sly grin.

"Oh, not too much," I said with an even slyer grin. "Not at first, anyway."

That sort of greedy talk might be frowned upon in most British circles, but I knew enough about the Spaniards by that time to have cottoned on to their admiration for someone who pulls a fast one. I mean, you only have to look at all the corruption that goes on in half the town halls in the country. Any bent mayors or councillors would probably get booed out of places in England, but in Spain people seemed to have a grudging respect for them, unless their thieving had affected them personally, in which case they were apt to dig out the old shotgun and wave it about a bit, especially the nutty old duffers in the villages.

I reeled in and examined my two worm-laden hooks, before casting out again. I'd seen blokes catch a few sea bream and the occasional sea bass from the spot where we were fishing, but I was quite happy to tighten the line and soak up a few benign winter rays.

"Frigiliana," Pedro said after a while.

"What's that? A fish?"

"Ha, no, it's a village a few kilometres down the coast, just inland a bit. It's a real tourist mecca and there are lots of arty shops there. It might be worth a visit."

"Hmm, thanks, Pedro, but I think we'll get our…" I was going to say 'little act going' before I remembered that Pedro wasn't necessarily going to be privy to Fede's transformation from bus-driving amateur dauber to enigmatic artist. "I think we'll save a place like that until we've made a start around here. Do you fancy a bit of breakfast?"

"Yes, there's nothing biting today."

When we'd finished our bocadillos, red wine with lemonade, and coffee in a nearby café, we had another couple of hours' fishing, or sitting in the sun, before it was time to join Doreen at the restaurant where our friend Juan worked. I would normally have been annoyed to find that she had invited her friend Janet plus husband Harvey along, but given recent developments I didn't mind too much.

Janet was a tall, slim woman who spoke Spanish about as well as I did, which wasn't too impressive for a former schoolteacher who'd lived there for about three years, but as she always knocked about with her lush of a husband or other British women, it wasn't surprising that she hadn't made more progress.

Harvey, the one with the mottled conk, was about my age but, despite his deep tan, which made his face look like a chocolate cake with a cherry, or raspberry, on top, a lifetime sat in offices had left him looking very flaccid, especially his wobbly cheeks. I wasn't sure how good his Spanish was, but he seemed to understand what I was saying to Pedro because he nodded a lot between forkfuls of rice and sips of wine.

I had managed to have a few quiet words with Doreen before we all sat down and I'd told her to pretend to know absolutely nothing about Fede.

"Why not, Ken?"

"Because he's not finished yet," I whispered.

"What do you mean?"

"Never mind, but just forget whatever I've told you about him. Wipe the slate clean."

"All right, Ken," she said, sensing that I was up to one of my cunning tricks, which I was, because I'd also had a word in Pedro's ear and told him much the same thing.

During that second bout of biteless fishing, you see, the wine and coffee must have stimulated my already active mind and Fede's transformation was beginning to take shape.

They talked about this and that during the main course – a seafood paella – but I said little, because I was running through all the European countries I could think of.

"Does anyone know anything about Albania?" I asked in English when we were tucking into our desserts. I spoke slowly, so that Pedro would understand me, as despite my efforts the conversation had switched to English.

"Why do you ask, Ken?" asked Doreen.

"Oh, it's just that when I was out walking the other day I met an Albanian bloke."

"Here in Fuentecastillo?" asked Janet.

"No, up in the hills," I said, waving vaguely towards the mountains. "He's living in a shack in the middle of nowhere and I stopped to have a word with him. Well, I tried to, because he only speaks a bit of Spanish."

As I spoke I saw Doreen's eyes widening and Pedro's narrowing, so I gave them both a solemn look in the hope that they'd control their facial muscles and not blurt out anything daft.

"What's he doing there?" asked Harvey.

"Painting."

"His shack?"

"No, pictures. Oil paintings. He showed me round inside. There were loads of paintings. I don't know much about art, but they looked pretty amazing to me."

"Perhaps we could drive out to see him one day," said Janet.

"No, he wouldn't like that. He's a hermit, you see." I looked at Pedro to check that he'd understood. He'd gone a bit red and was biting his lower lip, probably in an effort not to laugh, so I guessed he had.

"If he's a hermit, how come he spoke to you and invited you in?" asked Harvey in his drawly, clever sod voice.

"I don't know, Harvey. I guess he just liked the look of me, but he told me, in his very bad Spanish, that he didn't want me to tell anyone where he was."

"Does he not speak any English?" asked Doreen, having recovered her composure.

"No."

"French?" ask Janet in French.

"Nope, just a bit of Spanish. Anyway, he made some very bitter tea on an old camping stove and told me that he was an exile from Albania. He'd become quite famous there, but it seems that someone high up in the government didn't like his opinions, or his paintings, and they hounded him out," I said, resolving to get Doreen to look up Albania on the internet when we got home.

"How long has he been here?" asked Harvey, looking at me rather cynically from under his bushy grey eyebrows.

"About two years, I think. He had to leave all his paintings behind, but I think he brought a fair amount of money with him, so he rented the little house and has been painting there ever since."

"I thought you said it was a shack?" asked my inquisitor.

"To you and me it is," I said, having decided to make his residence sound a bit more believable. "But it's an old two-roomed house that some peasant probably used to live in. It's got electricity and he gets gas bottles from the village, as well as his food."

"Which village?"

"I'd rather not say, Harvey. He really doesn't want to be disturbed and if people find out what he's doing up there they won't leave him alone."

"What's he going to do with all his new paintings?" asked Doreen, earning herself a quick smile.

"Well, I'm not sure, but I *think* he was trying to tell me that he'll have to try to sell some, as his money's running out," I said, before asking Pedro if he'd understood.

"Yes, I understand, Ken," he said, before bowing his head and finishing off his flan.

"Juan's been too busy to stop to talk to us," I said, feeling that I'd said quite enough for one day.

"So what are you planning to do about this artist chappie, Ken?" asked Harvey, as I knew he would.

"Do? I don't plan to *do* anything. I just mentioned him in passing.

"Well, if it was me... I mean, if I was in this mysterious artist's confidence, I'd be thinking about helping him to sell some paintings," said Harvey with a shrewd look, spoilt only by the nose.

"Yes, Ken, it sounds like he'll struggle on his own," said Janet.

"And maybe you making little money too, eh?" said Pedro.

"Oh, we're all right for money," chipped in Doreen, having read my mind, "but I think you should go and see him again sometime and ask him if he needs any help."

"I might... Juan!" I said, hailing our waiter friend as he hurtled past. "Are they working you hard today," I added, in Spanish, of course.

"Sundays are always busy. Thank God it's my day off tomorrow."

"Are you free in the morning?"

"Yes."

"Let's meet up for a stroll and a bite to eat. There's something I want to tell you about."

"OK."

"I'll come to yours at about ten."

"OK, I must go now."

"How's your Albanian?" asked Pedro.

"What?"

"I'll explain tomorrow," I said as he hurried off to clear a table.

"What's all this Albania business, Ken?" asked Doreen as we were walking home some time later. We'd seen Pedro back to his car and I'd asked him to keep Fede under his hat for the time being, until I'd finalised the details and had them approved by the man himself.

"It's all part of the mystery," I said. "But you'd better look the place up on your computer when we get back. I think it's a good choice; you know, small and obscure, but I'd better find out a bit more about it."

"How does your friend Fede feel about being from Albania?"

"He doesn't know yet. I'd better give him a ring later."

"I thought Pedro was going to burst when you said it. How much does he know?"

"About as much as you, except I told him I was sure he was a genius," I said.

"And are you?"

"Doreen, I don't know the first thing about art, do I?"

"No, I forgot," she said, taking my arm, which I didn't mind as we were only two blocks from the flat. "It's all a bit confusing."

"It's all good fun."

"It's not like you, Ken."

"It is now," I said with a mischievous cackle. I pressed the lift button. "Now, go and switch that computer of yours on while I make us a cuppa."

# 7

By the time I met Juan the following morning – a rare overcast one – I'd gone a long way to creating the artistic personage of Fede, or rather Fisnik, which was his new name.

The night before, after reading about Albania and concluding that a poor country of only three million people had been a lucky choice, I called Fede to run my idea past him.

"What?" he said with astonishment, as I'd thought he might.

"I've thought it all through very carefully. Look, from what I can see, there's no shortage of artists trying to sell their paintings around here. If they think you're a misunderstood genius, forced to leave your country, it'll generate a lot of interest."

"Ken, I don't think–"

"You haven't signed any of your paintings yet, have you?"

"No."

"Good. You're called Fisnik now."

"What?"

"Fisnik. As it sounds, with a K on the end. You don't have any surnames."

"No?"

"No, we'll keep it simple, and enigmatic. Fisnik means gallant, generous and noble," I said, hoping he would be all those things when the time came to discuss money.

"My wife won't like it, or the bus company," he said, which just shows how naïve my pal was.

"Ha, think of it as a stage name. You just carry on as normal and when we go off selling paintings you become Fisnik."

"I don't speak Albanian."

"Me neither, but we'll learn a few phrases. You won't speak much Spanish either, in fact you won't be saying much at all. All you have to do is sit there looking like a genius in your cape and hat."

"My what?"

"Cape and hat. My wife ordered them from England last night. It's a handy thing the internet. They're nice old ones, and I've got you some dark glasses too, little round ones. We'll get you some pointed shoes too."

"This all sounds a bit crazy, Ken. What if we get found out?"

"Who cares? We'll say it was a joke. Either way you'll get known and be able to sell some paintings. I've printed out some photos too, so you can paint a few scenes from Tirana, from memory."

"What's that?"

"Your native city, which you were expelled from about two years ago. Let's meet tomorrow evening in the bar and I'll tell you all about yourself."

"All right, Ken," he said in a resigned sort of way.

"Remember, Fisnik, it's just a bit of fun."

"All right, Ken. Will you be dressing up too?"

"Possibly. Hasta mañana."

I could see that there was still quite a bit of spadework to do with Fede/Fisnik, but having been given a greenish light, I lost no time in telling Juan about my plan. If you've read Doreen's little book you'll know that Juan's a resourceful young chap who speaks English fairly well and I rather wanted to get him in on the act.

"So that's the story so far," I said over our breakfast at a quiet bar near the sea. "I really think he's a great painter, but this will help him to make an impact."

"It sounds like fun, but I can see a problem," he said, having heard about as much as you've read.

"What's that?"

"Well, if Fede lives here he might be spotted by those English friends of yours. Perhaps you should tell them the truth too."

"No, I can't do that, because they're the ones who're going to spread the story. In any case, I don't think Fede gets around much, except to the bar where we meet, and they'll not see him there."

"But he's a bus driver. Lots of people catch the bus to Málaga rather than driving in."

"He doesn't do that route. He goes to Málaga by car and drives the buses from there. He's doing the Málaga to Seville route at the moment, I think."

"That's all right then. I'm driving up to the village to see my mother now. Do you want to come?"

"Not today, Juan, but tell whoever you see that a famous Albanian painter might soon be in town."

"Ha, I will."

"And mention him at the restaurant too, if you get the chance."

"OK."

"There'll be ten percent of each sale that you help to make for you," I said, resolving to tell Fede about my subagents that evening.

"You can count on me, Ken."


"What's all this about, Ken?" Fede asked me that evening as I led him to the quietest table in the bar with a bottle of beer in each hand.

I explained my reasoning again and reassured him that he would only have to put on his Albanian artist act when we went off to sell paintings.

"Only then?"

"Only then, Fede."

"So about once a week?"

"Yes, if that, and not for a while yet."

"I'm still not keen on the idea," he said, though he looked nowhere near as despondent as he'd sounded on the phone the previous evening.

"Look, Fede, in an area like this, with so many foreigners and people from other parts of Spain, there are lots of artists trying to sell paintings," I said.

"I know, but most of them are no good."

"Maybe so, but the public doesn't know that. Your Albanian act, as well as your great skill, will make all the difference."

"But I don't want to be this Fisnik chap forever. I have my artistic integrity to consider," he said, slurping from his bottle in a most inartistic way.

"Think about Dalí."

"What about him?"

"Well, he did all sorts of crazy things, didn't he?"

"Yes, he once filled a Rolls Royce with cauliflower."

"There you are then," I said.

"We're not going to do anything like that, are we?"

"No, no need for cauliflower. The point is that if we get found out–"

"*When* we get found out, Ken."

"If or when we get found out, we just say it was an artistic stunt. You can say you were so fascinated by the place that you started to feel Albanian."

"I've hardly heard of Albania."

"Maybe not, but you'll soon have some paintings to prove that you've been there," I said, placing three printed photos of Tirana on the table.

"Hmm," he said, eyeing the photos.

"Like Dalí, one stunt can lead to another, you see. How soon do you think you can do a small painting of each of these?"

"They don't inspire me, Ken, and I never paint from photos," he said, looking at the two cityscapes and a funny church. "I can't paint these tower blocks, but I suppose I could do one of this church. I like the big dome."

"It's orthodox, I think. How about a mosque too? There'll be plenty of those, as more than half of them are Muslims. How do you fancy being a Muslim artist?"

"No, Ken. I'd be expected to go off and pray and there are quite a few Moroccans around here who'd see through me."

"Good thinking. You can be an atheist then. Miremengjes, Fisnik."

"What?"

"It means good morning in Albanian. Miremengjes. You say it."

"Miremengjes."

"Excellent."

"Though it's not morning."

"It's the only thing I've been able to memorise. I'll try to learn a couple more things."

"What if we see some Albanians, Ken?"

"What are the chances of that? I've never met one."

"Me neither." He picked up the photo of the church. "I'll make a start on this tomorrow night."

"Great. Just a small one will do. It's just to cry over really."

"Cry over?"

"Well, you know, look all sad and homesick. They'll be your most expensive paintings, as it'd break your heart to part with them. Another beer?"

"Vale."

After his fourth beer Fede began to warm to my little deception and asked me when he'd be making his debut.

"It depends on how fast I can generate some interest. I've got two local friends working on that, and my wife's going to make sure lots of foreigners know about you," I said, before mentioning that certain people would have to be offered a financial incentive.

"I'll leave that side of things up to you, Ken. After all, I've made exactly zero from my paintings so far and I had no real prospects of selling any until I met you."

"How long does it take you to paint one?"

"Oh, anywhere from a few hours to a month."

"It might be as well to do some rapid ones so we don't run out," I said, ever the optimist.

"I can do small ones quite quickly, especially if I base them on others I've done," he said, a promising glint of avarice appearing in his eyes.

"Try to do quite a few in the next week or two then. I'd better go now."

"Shall we meet here on Wednesday?"

"We can't."

"Why not?"

"Because you'll be busy painting."

"Right, I don't mind that. I'll tell my wife that I'll soon be selling some."

"Hmm, can you trust her not to gossip?"

"If she thinks there'll be money in it, she'll be a tomb," he said, which means keeping your trap shut in Spanish.

During the following fortnight I wore my thinking cap permanently, even in bed, it seemed, as I dreamt up new ideas almost every night. I decided against a catalogue in the end, because how does a refugee living in a shack in the middle of nowhere get round to publishing one of those? I could say I'd done it, of course, but when we finally made our debut I didn't want to seem *too* involved in Fisnik's management.

No, I would be merely a generous-spirited helper who had put his car at Fisnik's disposal, being the only person that the shy genius could bring himself to communicate with. I would explain to potential customers that as well as helping Fisnik to move out of his unhealthy hovel, they would also be investing their money wisely, as he would soon be as famous in Spain as he was in Albania.

So, with that double-pronged sales pitch – stressing either philanthropy or gain, depending on who I was talking to – all that remained was to set up a viewing to which a few sympathetic punters would be sure to come.

# 8

"Do you like it here, dear," I said to Doreen the following Sunday as we ate alone at a nice restaurant just down the coast.

"It's lovely. So thoughtful of you to have brought me, Ken." She grasped my forearm and I didn't budge it.

"Is the word about Fisnik spreading fast, do you think?"

"I think so. Janet, Mildred and Barbara keep asking when he'll be showing his paintings and I tell them that it all depends on you persuading him to leave his shack and brave the eyes of the world, just like you told me to."

"That's good. Are they telling other people about him?"

"Everyone they see. He's the talk of the town; well, among the expats."

"Great. Let's have a really nice bottle of wine today."

"Can Fede not show his paintings here in Fuentecastillo?"

"You mean Fisnik? No, not here."

"That's a pity, because it would be easier to get people to go."

"Yes, and easier for someone to say, 'Hello, this Fisnik looks an awful lot like that bus driver chap who I've seen around town.' It's too risky. I think we'll start up in the village where we used to live."

"Where exactly?"

"Juan's been talking to the owner of the restaurant where he used to work. They close on Tuesdays now and Juan thinks he can persuade him to open just for an exhibition. Juan would run the bar, so the owners would make some money on their day off. Pedro says he'll help out too, and he'll tell everybody about it, especially the foreigners."

"Will he get a cut too?"

"Everyone who does anything will get a cut. That's business, after all."

"Harvey says he wants a commission if he finds any buyers."

"He would, and he'll get one. He's still suspicious about the whole thing, but a bit of cash will ease his doubts."

"Will I get a cut?"

"Not you, Doreen, no."

"Aw," she said, slapping my hand playfully, though it stung all the same.

"You won't need one, because Fede will be generous with me, especially when things get moving."

"Are you sure?"

"Yes, he's a good bloke and it's all my doing, after all."

"I still haven't met him."

"And you won't, only as Fisnik. It's better that way. I haven't seen much of him lately as he's painting like mad. I took him those church photos you printed round to his flat yesterday and he was up at the house, or rather shack, ha ha. I hope the cape, hat and glasses arrive soon."

"They should come this week."

"I have to buy him some pointy black shoes too. Size forty-three. All being well, Fisnik will be launched a week on Tuesday."

"Here's to Fisnik," she said, raising her glass.

"Yes, to Fisnik, and prosperity."

"We're prosperous anyway, Ken."

"Yes, but a bit more won't do us any harm, and it's all in the name of art."

When I started this book I didn't mean it to be *all* about the Fisnik phenomenon, but I guess it did sort of take over from about February onwards and all my usual activities paled into insignificance. The restaurant owner in the village dragged his feet a bit, but as my mother's visit was imminent I decided to postpone the first ever Albanian art exhibition in the area until the last Tuesday of the month.

My old Mum, who's eighty-four but very fit for her age, enjoyed her stay and it gave me a bit of time for reflection before our show hit the road. Apart from the smell of Brussel sprouts throughout the flat – which annoyed Doreen more than it did me, as I quite like them – it wasn't a bad week, but I couldn't dismantle the bed fast enough when she'd gone and reinstall my comfy chair and little table. I'd put Fede's little picture up in that room, as a source of inspiration for our future endeavours, though I planned to invest in a few of his weird ones too, before the prices went through the roof.

"Buenos días," I said to Fede on arriving at his very spruce little 'shack' on the Sunday morning before our first exhibition.

"Miremengjes, Ken."

"What?"

"Have you forgotten already?"

"Er... oh, miremengjes to you too. I haven't got round to learning any more, I'm afraid."

"Emri im eshte Fisnik. Unë jam nga Tirana."

"What?"

"I'm Fisnik. I'm from Tirana."

"Bloody hell," I said in English.

"Is that Albanian too?"

"No, that's English for being very surprised."

"I learnt it from the internet," he said proudly. "I know a few more things too, like how to say I like and don't like things."

"Great, that's one less thing for me to worry about. So I guess you're feeling a bit more optimistic about everything?"

"Yes, it was painting the churches that gave me a feel for the place. I've printed some more photos out, some of a village and others of snowy mountains. What do you think of this?" he showed me a small, half-finished canvas of some very swirly, snowy mountains.

"That's great, Fede."

"And what do you think of these?" He showed me a strip of canvas with Fisnik written in about a dozen different ways.

"Er, how about this one?" I said, pointing to a slightly gothic looking version that he'd done twice.

"Yes, that's my favourite too. It's going to feel strange writing it on my paintings, though."

"Just put it on the ones that we'll be taking with us on Tuesday. Was there any problem getting the day off?"

"Hospital appointment," he said without a flicker of doubt. "Let's have some breakfast." He made for the little kitchen.

"I'd rather have breakfast with Fisnik," I said, handing him a big shopping bag. "I'll make the bocadillos while you put all this on. We'll meet on the patio and have a trial run."

Ten minutes later I'd knocked up a couple of cured ham and cheese butties and taken them outside. I was just pouring out the red wine and lemonade when Fisnik made his first appearance, resplendent in his black cape and unusual hat. Instead of going for a beret, which would have been a bit too stereotypical, Doreen had helped me to find a black suede cap on the internet, a bit like the flat caps my old Dad used to wear, but a bit more bulgy on top, to leave room for his enormous brain.

"Miremengjes, Ken."

"Miremengjes, Fisnik," I said, taking him in from top to toe. The ample cap was a gem, the well-worn cape was perfect, and the pointy shoes just right.

"What do you think?" he asked in halting Spanish.

"Very good, Fisnik, apart from the jeans. I think you need a black shirt and trousers, not too new," I said, even more slowly than I usually spoke in Spanish.

"Black shirt have. Black trousers also," he said, speaking a bit like I did, but with a funny accent that I thought would do as well as any other.

"Good. Oh, the glasses."

Once he'd put on the little round sunglasses and wrapped the cape around him, the picture was complete. I'd toyed with the idea of getting him a false beard, but thought that might be going a bit too far, and that someone like Harvey might cotton onto it. Besides, with the cap covering his stubbly, greying hair, he looked quite different.

Then he said something unintelligible.

"What's that?"

"I like wine, in Albanian."

"Brilliant. Tuesday's going to be a big success."

"Slowly, please. My Spanish is too bad."

"Right, yes, let's get into our roles."

For the rest of the morning I spoke bad, slow Spanish, which was second nature to me, and Fede spoke terrible, even slower Spanish, throwing in a bit of Albanian now and then from the crib sheet he'd printed. We selected twenty paintings for our first exhibition and spaced them out along the living room walls.

On picking up one of a multi-coloured, swirling, orthodox church, he began to croon softly to himself, before shaking his head and burying his face in his hands.

"One day you will go back, Fisnik," I said, patting him on the back.

"Oh, my country!" he wailed, squeezing his eyes together and producing a couple of real tears.

"Poor Fisnik," I said, addressing a hypothetical bystander in English. "He can't go back, but if at least he could live in a decent house here... so sad."

We moved on to a larger painting of a Spanish village scene.

"Happy, happy village," he said, smiling now. "Happy, happy people in Spain."

"Come outside to rest, Fisnik, while these nice people look at your paintings."

"Happy, happy people," he murmured, nodding to them as he followed me outside with stooped shoulders and a shuffling gait.

We kept up the act for a while longer and ran through a couple of hypothetical scenarios, before taking a breather.

"A small beer, Fisnik?"

"Yes, but let's stop now, Ken. It's hard work for me."

"OK. Who'd have thought you'd have got into your part so well, eh?"

"It's sort of grown on me, Ken, and, I mean, life can get a bit dull, just driving and painting all the time," he said, before furrowing his brow, a bit like Fisnik. "We won't get into trouble, will we?"

"What do you mean?"

"Well, for fraud or something."

"Only if there's another Albanian painter called Fisnik around."

"Unlikely."

"Yes. Here's to Tuesday," I said, raising my glass.

"Të marten," he said, clinking his glass against mine.

"That's a bit like Spanish."

"Po."

"Sí?"

"Sí."

# 9

As Fede, Juan and Pedro had all taken the day off work, I was keen for our first exhibition to go well. I didn't expect miracles, of course, but I hoped to get a little money into all their pockets before the end of the day, especially Fede's. He looked a bit anxious when I picked him up at eight.

"Miremengjes, Fisnik."

"Buenos días, Ken. Let's not start the act until I've got changed. I'm a bit nervous."

"Well, looking nervous won't be a bad thing. You are a hermit, after all."

By half past eight we'd driven to the house, loaded the bubble-wrapped, signed paintings into the back of my car, and Fede had become Fisnik; cape, cap, glasses, pointy shoes and all. I was dressed normally as I was merely his driver and only friend.

"You look very good, Fisnik," I said.

"I speak little today, Ken," he said in his funny accent.

"Yes, the less you speak, the less can go wrong."

"Too fast, Ken. I no understand."

"That's the spirit. Now, when we arrive, I think it's best if you stay in the car for a bit while me, Juan and Pedro unwrap and arrange the paintings."

"OK."

"Are you happy with the prices we've decided on?"

"Yes. Expensive, but good."

At my insistence, we had priced the pictures between €100 for the small, Spanish ones and €450 for the small Albanian ones, which was a bit ironic as he'd knocked those off from the photos quite quickly. Most of the larger Spanish ones were around the three to four hundred mark, so anyone looking for a bargain would have to go for one of the smaller exhibits. I'd been inclined to price a few even higher, until Fede pointed out that there was a limit to how much you could take out at a cashpoint.

"Expensive, yes," I said, "but remember there'll be ten percent for Juan and ten for Pedro, and maybe a bit for any of my wife's friends who bring anyone who buys."

"And you, Ken?" he asked, sticking to his role.

"Nothing for me today," I said, thinking that quite enough slices of the pie were going to be dished out. "If it goes well we can talk about that later, but I'm not too bothered."

"We speak later. Now I closing eyes. This road very…"

"Twisty?"

"Yes."

I slowed down a bit, as the last thing I wanted was for Fisnik to be sick on his lovely cape, but the inevitable tractor, which had been Doreen's nemesis when we lived up there, soon came into view, so we were down to a snail's pace for the last few miles.

The exhibition, for which Pedro had made some very rustic posters and festooned the village with them, was due to open at ten, so we had plenty of time to stack up most of the chairs, push the tables against the walls, and display all twenty painting, which I must say did look quite impressive under the bright restaurant lights. We didn't put any refreshments out, as that was what the bar was for, and if we were to be allowed to use the place again we'd be as well to make a tidy sum for the owner, who would be popping in later on.

"Is your friend going to come in?" asked Juan as he made us coffees.

"I'll go and see."

A few moments later Fisnik shuffled into the restaurant and smiled bashfully at Juan and Pedro. I'd told him to stick to his role even with my friends, to prevent any blunders later on.

"I'm Pedro, pleased to meet you," he said, extending his hand.

"I am Fisnik," said Fisnik with a shy smile, his hands holding his cape around him. He peered at his pictures through his dark glasses and nodded with approval.

Juan came around the bar and greeted him.

"I am Fisnik. Happy be here. Ken friends my friends," he said in his guttural accent. He'd told me earlier that he'd actually listened to a bit of Albanian on the computer, so I was becoming more and more impressed by that alien invention.

"Ha, you really look and sound the part... Fede, isn't it?" said Juan.

"I am Fisnik. Better I am Fisnik always."

"I suppose so. Do you want a coffee... Fisnik?"

"Please, with little brandy."

After knocking back his stimulant he walked round the exhibition, adjusting a picture or two.

"I go car now, Ken. When some people here, I come."

"OK, Fisnik."

I watched Juan and Pedro watching him shuffle out.

"What do you think, lads?"

"He'd convince me," said Pedro.

"Has he done any acting before?" asked Juan.

"I don't think so, but he's an artist, so he's pretty creative," I said.

"I'd like to meet the real man, too," said Pedro.

"Maybe later when we're counting up the money," I said with a greedy cackle. "What about a bit of music, Juan? Are there any Albanian CDs back there?"

"Ha, I doubt it." He shuffled through the rack. "How about some classical?"

"Definitely."

"Bach?"

I woofed, explained the joke, and gave the thumbs up to the soothing but stimulating tones. You can't beat a bit of Bach.

When the CD ended about an hour later the absence of punters was becoming a cause for concern. I checked on the main attraction and found him snoozing, so I returned inside and borrowed Pedro's mobile phone.

"Doreen, where are you?" I asked my tardy wife.

"Behind a tractor, of course. We'll be there soon."

"Are there many people coming."

"Wait and see."

"A few?"

"Tell Juan to line up the coffee saucers."

Sure enough, a short time later not only had Doreen, Janet, Harvey, Mildred, Geoffrey and Barbara arrived, but also a bevy of other Fuentecastillo expats. By the time they'd all found somewhere to park and wandered in, there were about twenty of them, and Juan was sliding coffees across the bar one after another, as well as a few beers and wines for the early starters, like Harvey and Geoffrey.

There was quite a buzz as they milled around looking at the paintings, and I thought it was about time Fisnik made an appearance so that they'd see who had created those strange, rather expensive works of art.

He'd woken up by that time and the sight of all the foreigners trooping into the restaurant had given his tanned face quite an artistic pallor.

"Are you ready to make your grand entrance, Fisnik?" I asked on opening the car door.

"Shit, Ken, I didn't expect so many people," he said, sounding more like Fede than Fisnik.

"It's good if you're nervous. I'll tell them you're not used to seeing people."

His anxiety made his entrance a convincing one. He surveyed the scene with awe, nodded shyly to a few people, and shuffled over to a chair in the corner.

"A drink, Fisnik?" I asked, making a drinking motion.

"Small brandy, please."

I got him his brandy, patted him on the shoulder, and stood between him and the throng, which now included a few curious locals. Harvey was the first to approach, which I didn't mind as it was as well to get the doubting Thomas out of the way first.

"Can I meet the great man, Ken?" he asked, glass of red wine in hand.

"Just say hello if you want. He's very nervous. He hasn't seen so many people since he left Albania.

"Hmm." He peered at the resting genius through red-rimmed eyes. "Hello, I am Harvey," he said in the drawling Spanish that Home Counties folk tend to speak.

"Fisnik," said Fisnik from his chair, with a total lack of expression on his face.

"Your pictures are very interesting."

"Yes."

"Your use of colour is... original."

Blank stare from Fisnik, made all the blanker by the dark glasses.

"Do you always paint in oils?"

At this, Fisnik adjusted his cap, bowed his head, and didn't look like he was going to lift it again until this unwelcome presence had departed.

"I don't think he likes me," Harvey said to me.

"Oh, I don't think it's that, but, as I told you, he's a hermit and this is all a bit much for him. He didn't want to come at all, really, but I persuaded him."

"Hmm, well I'll not be buying any of the ignorant devil's daubings," he said, before marching back to the bar.

I didn't think this the best of starts, and whispered as much to the artist when he'd gone.

"Not so bad, Ken. Different people, different Fisnik. You will see."

"I hope you're right."

There was plenty of milling going on, but I was anxious for someone to buy a picture and set an example to the rest. Fede and I had rehearsed how payment would be taken and we'd agreed that it ought to cause quite a stir. Just then I saw Hella, the Swedish woman who had helped us with our paperwork when we'd first moved to the village, so I strode over to greet her.

"Hi, Hella, nice to see you here."

"You too, Ken. I didn't know you were an art connoisseur," she said with an ironic Nordic smirk.

"Well, I know a genius when I see one."

"The paintings are certainly interesting, especially the ones of the strange churches."

"They're his most treasured works, done from his fond memories of his homeland," I said solemnly. Hella was a sharp one and was as much a test as Harvey in her way.

"Well, as there are no men here worth knowing, I will study the pictures once more."

"They're a good investment," I said, conscious of her fondness for money.

"Maybe."

The next old face I saw was that of Shirley, our miserly ex-neighbour in the village. She was talking earnestly to Doreen, probably angling for an invite to lunch, so I just waved because the likelihood of her buying a picture was practically nil.

When I turned to check on Fisnik, I saw that a short, stout, middle-aged lady with dyed blonde hair and toasted skin was talking to him and getting a far better reception than Harvey had. I sidled closer to eavesdrop.

"Yes, I like you pictures very much," she was saying, her Spanish sounding a bit West Country. That's how bad most Brits speak it, you see, and I think us gruff northerners carry it off better than most.

"Gracias, gracias, gracias," said Fisnik, in his strong Albanian accent. He was still seated, but was smiling broadly and moving his head from side to side in a strange but endearing way.

"Which pictures do you enjoy painting the most?" she asked him.

Still smiling, he shrugged, so I stepped in.

"His Spanish isn't very good, I'm afraid," I said in English. "I'm Ken, Fisnik's friend."

"Hi, I'm Muriel. How did you meet him?"

I told her the story of our chance encounter outside his shack, the cup of bitter tea, his slowly warming to me, me being his only contact with the outside world, and more things like that, which I'd rehearsed in my head a thousand times.

"So you're his manager, then?"

"No, nothing like that. Just a friend. I want to help him move out of the awful place where he's living and rent a decent little flat or house. He doesn't want to sell his paintings, but I've explained that it's the only way," I said, before looking at Fisnik with an expression I usually reserved for little puppies, which bring out my softer side.

"Poor man. Has he sold any yet?"

"No, everybody's enjoying the pictures, but nobody seems to be buying."

"Well let's set an example, shall we? I'll choose one. Who do I pay?"

"Pay Fisnik, please. Thank you, it'll make him so happy."

The lady, for a lady she was, strode over to the tables and surveyed our wares. She hovered before a small picture of a Spanish church that looked like it had spent some time in a washing machine, but finally plumped for a medium-sized one of a Spanish village which could have been Pompeii when the lava oozed into town.

I whipped some bubble wrap from under a table and hurried to her side.

"A fine choice, Muriel. Fisnik will be ever so pleased."

To say that Fisnik was pleased was an understatement. As we approached him, me with the picture and Muriel with her purse in hand, he rose slowly to his feet, before stretching his arms wide, making him look like a gigantic crow. He raised his hands slowly upwards, before uttering a long, incomprehensible sentence in a loud, high-pitched voice. I won't try to reproduce it here, but Fede had assured me that it meant, 'Every man is the smith of his own fortune,' and it sounded even better than when he'd rehearsed it the previous Sunday.

Having got the attention of everybody, including a couple of schoolkids who must have been passing, he then proceeded to fall slowly to his knees, bringing his hands together as he did so to collect the cash (€280), before leaning forward and kissing each of Muriel's shoes.

When he'd kissed my sandals two days earlier, we couldn't decide how best to end the party piece, but after a few false starts we'd settled on the only thing we could think of which wouldn't be an anti-climax.

So, before Muriel had time to look embarrassed, which wouldn't have done, Fisnik sprang to his feet, hugged her briefly, and raced out of the door, clearly on the point of tears. The astonishment was absolute. I'd been afraid that some insensitive soul like Harvey might burst out laughing, so while silence reigned I hurried out to attend to the emotional maestro.

I wasn't surprised or displeased to see several people following me to my nearby car, and Fisnik's foolproof finale was every bit as effective as we'd thought it would be. He'd locked himself in the car and was sitting with head bowed, a teary streak on each of his cheeks (produced by a little spittle).

I tried the door, to no avail.

"We'd better leave him for a while," I said to my fellow sympathisers. "I'm sure he'll come back in when he's ready."

As we walked away, only Harvey stayed put, but as I knew that my friend was counting to five hundred, it was unlikely that the cynic would be able to stay away from the bar for so long.

After that little drama, just about the best entertainment anyone could hope for on a cloudy Tuesday morning in a village in the hills of Malaga, no-one seemed inclined to leave the exhibition.

Doreen approached me and expressed her concern.

"He'll be all right, love. It was just a bit much for him."

"You pair of devils," she whispered.

"Careful," I said, patting her arm.

"He's not one of these aloof artists, then," said Harvey on his return.

The lack of sarcasm in his voice made me think that we just might have cracked it.

# 10

A single chapter can't possibly do justice to the events of that day, and as the restless murmuring that ensued was a bit like half-time, I'll start a new one.

A few minutes later Fisnik returned, bestowing little bows and shy smiles as he made his way to his chair in the corner.

"A drink, Fisnik?" I asked him, risking a quick wink.

"Small brandy, please. How I do?" he murmured.

"Great."

Most of the art lovers were on the wine and beer by this time, and the volume of chatter increased as more people entered. Some were local expats, and a few were real locals who Pedro took under his wing and showed around. People often turned to look at Fisnik, who sat cradling his brandy glass, his face wearing a blank expression once more, and there was a great sense of expectation as everybody waited for somebody else to buy a painting.

When Doreen's friend Barbara picked up a small picture of a seascape that Turner might have done after a liquid lunch, I saw a few cameras and mobile phones being slipped out of pockets and handbags.

"Shall I wrap it for you, Barbara?" I asked her.

"Please, Ken, but could you take the money? I don't want to upset him again."

"I'm afraid not, Barbara. It's bad luck in Albania not to handle the money from a sale. I'll come over with you."

The fact that Barbara had only chosen a €100 picture made no difference at all to Fisnik's celebration of the deal, which was identical to the treatment that Muriel had received, only this time it was accompanied by several camera flashes. The only slight modification was that, once he'd dextrously pocketed the cash, he walked rather than ran out of the room, shadowing his already obscured eyes with his hand.

Me and a few other people stepped outside, but on seeing Fisnik in the car with the seat reclined we left him in peace. There was another lull, but when Fisnik returned, bowing and smiling, the punters' pleasure was palpable and they were soon supping and chattering again.

Aware that alcohol can do much to loosen the purse strings, although it's never loosened mine, I wandered over to Fede, who seemed to be in a trance, and ran my idea past him.

"Yes, Ken, but just beer or wine, so the owner won't notice," he said, quite the ventriloquist.

I then clapped my hands and made an announcement.

"Fisnik would like to express his gratitude to you for coming to see his humble paintings by inviting you all to a glass of beer or wine."

The maestro greeted the murmur of approval by standing, bowing stiffly, and resuming his seat. Pedro joined Juan behind the bar and they despatched the drinks quickly. I even had a caña myself, as all that chatting was thirsty and unfamiliar work.

Next to buy and get the Fisnik treatment was a young local lady, who chose a small painting of a multi-coloured mountain, which she swore was the one she saw from her balcony, and she had a friend standing by with a camera to capture the celebration ritual.

On Fisnik's return from the car, a bloke who might have been Dutch or German bought another small one, of some blob-like children near a fountain, and I guessed that for some folk it was worth €100 just to get their feet kissed.

An elderly, soldierly, English chap who had been drinking with Harvey and Geoffrey picked up a small painting of the Albanian church, before putting it down when he saw the hefty price tag. He moved along and studied the biggest picture of all. Fede had told me that it was of the village near his little house, painted from the mountainside. It was good in its way, though the houses appeared to have melted. The man called me over.

"Shall I wrap it for you?" I asked.

"Hmm, I rather fancied that one of the curious church," he said in one of those fruity voices that I usually hated but didn't mind so much just then. "But if this big one's the same price, I think I'll take it. It'll look well in my study."

"A good choice, and just as well, really. I don't know how he'll react if anyone buys one of his Albanian ones."

"No?"

"No, they're very dear to him and he's quite an emotional man."

"Yes, I can see that. Rum chappie," he said, glancing from Fisnik to the picture of the church.

"Mind you, he says he's not going to paint any more Albanian pictures, as he finds it too traumatic, so they might be worth quite a bit soon."

"Hmm, that's true," said the half-cut old duffer. "I shall just pop out to the bank."

Five minutes later he was back with a wad of notes clasped in his hand. "Harriet!" he called to his wife, who scurried over. "Immortalise this moment for me on film on that little device of your, won't you?"

"Yes, dear," she chirped, looking wistfully at his clenched fist.

As I approached Fisnik I held up the little painting and pulled aside the bubble wrap. He peered at me over his glasses and appeared to steel himself. He rose slowly from his chair, but instead of raising his arms prior to hollering his little catchphrase, he stood transfixed by the picture. When compete silence had fallen he slowly raised his arms.

"Albania, Shqipëri, Albania, Shqipëri! he yelled, the funny word meaning Albania in Albanian, before kissing the man on both cheeks, kissing the picture, falling to his knees and taking the cash, giving the man's feet the old one-two, jumping to his feet, and hurtling out of the restaurant with arms raised, wailing, "Atdheu im, atdheu im, atdheu im!"

"I think that means 'my homeland', I said to the stunned ex-officer.

"Did you film that, Harriet?" he asked his wife in a trembling voice.

"Oh, yes."

"That'll be something to show 'em back at the club," he said as he trudged back towards the bar.

"Don't forget this, sir," I said, handing him the painting.

"My, my," he muttered, smiling and shaking his head.

That was a hard act to follow, even for Fisnik, who remained in the car for a whole quarter hour. When he returned there were three people ready to buy Spanish paintings, so he included them all in the same ceremony, before staggering outside.

His stagger had been so convincing that I popped out to see if he was all right.

"I don't think I can take much more today, Ken," he said, there being nobody else around. "That Albanian painting really got to me."

"What do you mean?"

"It almost broke my heart to part with it."

"But you're not even Albanian, Fede," I said, using his real name in order to bring him back to reality.

"I know, I know, but I could almost see myself walking past that church on my way to exile."

"Bloody hell, Fede," I said, as he already knew what that meant. "Come in one more time and I'll tell them we're finishing soon."

It was only half past one, but a few people were beginning to leave and I thought it best not to let things peter out, so I walked around telling everybody that we'd be closing at two.

"When will there be another exhibition?" a Scotchman (sic) asked me.

"I can't say for sure. It depends how Fisnik feels after today. If he's prepared to do another, we'll put up some posters a week or two before."

"He's a phenomenon."

"Yes."

"And his paintings are something special. You can see the emotion he puts into them."

"Yes, you can," I said to the tipsy chap. "He paints very slowly."

"I'd better buy one."

"Yes, I would."

He paid €240 for the one of the old woman, joining Hella, who bought a small Spanish one, in what I thought would be the last wailing, kissing and scarpering ceremony of the day. Then Harvey approached me.

"Ken, I talked old Bob into splashing out on that Albanian picture. Do I get my ten percent?"

"Well, Harvey, I don't know…"

"If I do, I'll buy that last little Spanish one."

"Really?"

"Yes, but I don't want any of that foot kissing business, so here's €55 if you'll keep it for me."

"All right," I said, turning the picture of a flock of blue and pink sheep to face the wall.

"A sound investment, eh?"

"Yes, get some food inside you before you drive back down that road."

"Janet's driving," he said, before shambling back to the bar.

And that was that. At two o'clock we locked the door and the four of us sat down at a table that Pedro had pulled over into Fisnik's corner, having let down the blinds on the nearby windows. We remained silent for a while, sipping beer and nibbling nuts, waiting for Fisnik to break the spell.

After a long swig of beer he stood up, took off his cap, glasses and cape, and sat down again.

"F*ck me, that was hard work," he said, or words to that effect.

"Are you Fede again now?" asked Juan, also looking pretty drained after his nonstop bar work.

"Yes, thank God. Pleased to meet you both." He shook hands with Juan and Pedro.

"I think that was a success," I said, looking over at the few remaining paintings.

"It was," said Fede, before standing to empty his trouser pockets. "Who would have thought." We looked at the pile of banknotes. "You count it, Ken. I'm too tired."

I soon totted up our takings. "€1,905," I announced proudly, before pushing the notes over to Fede.

Without a glance at any of us, he counted off some notes and thrust them back into his pocket. There were a lot left on the table.

"You divide that thousand between you as you see fit," he said.

"Whoa, Fede," I said, sounding very English. "That's far too much."

"Too much," echoed Juan, licking his lips.

"Ten percent is more than enough for me," said Pedro.

"And this," said Fede, patting his pocket, "is more than enough for me. A month ago I hadn't a thought of selling my paintings. It's all thanks to Ken, and you two."

"You painted them, Fede," I said.

"That little Albanian one that the tall, red man bought for €450 took me two hours to paint. I'm more than happy."

"Three ways then," I said to my two helpers.

In the end they twisted my arm and I pocketed four hundred, while they divided the rest.

Just then there was a knock on the door. Fede went to hide in the bathroom and Juan opened up for the owner. He was delighted with the takings on his day off and insisted that we left everything just as it was.

"My wife and I will clean and prepare the restaurant tomorrow morning. Please bring the key round later, Pedro," he said, and was off.

We had a couple more beers and a bite to eat.

"Where to next then, Fede?" I asked after nipping out for a smoke.

"I don't know, Ken. I'm not sure I can do it again."

"Well, that's up to you, of course," I said, getting a sinking feeling after all the excitement.

"It's true that if you don't do another exhibition, this one will become legendary," said Pedro.

"Maybe you could do one more in Fuentecastillo to cement your reputation," said Juan.

"Not there. Too risky," said Fede, looking so different to Fisnik that I was almost sure no-one would recognise him.

"It's a good idea to just do one more, though, maybe in another village" I said. "After that you could become a hermit again and just sell your paintings through us."

"We'll see. Thank you all for your help. Today has been... memorable."

# 11

Life went back to normal for a while after that.

The next time I met Fede, about a week later in our usual bar, he told me that he didn't want to talk about Fisnik or exhibitions for a while.

"I need some time to think," he said.

"OK. Are you still painting?"

"Yes, but I'm not going to sign any more for now."

"Did you tell your wife about the exhibition?"

"More or less. I gave her most of the money though, so now *she* wants me to do another one too," he said, looking stressed.

"Not another word then. Pedro's coming down to fish next Sunday if you fancy a change."

"I might, but he'll be thinking about the Fisnik thing too, even if he doesn't mention it."

"Hmm, it was exciting though, and you were brilliant. Things like that don't happen every day."

"I know why actors get nervous every time they go on stage now. I used to wonder why they didn't get used to it."

"Look, Málaga are playing tonight."

"Yes, let's watch a bit of football."


As I sit here now in my little room with my pen and notepad, I think I feel a bit like Doreen did when she reached the point in her story when we had moved down here and everything was hunky-dory. The next few weeks were the calm *after* the storm, and a pretty dull calm it seemed too.

I mean, I did my walks along the beach, drank my coffees and beers, and generally pottered around enjoying the improving weather, but it always seemed like something was missing. But don't worry, I'm not going to wind up the story quickly like Doreen did, as there's still more to tell.

She was out socialising as much as ever, but she was getting tired of everyone asked when Fisnik was going to do his next exhibition.

"Can you not persuade him to appear again, Ken?" she asked me one mild evening in late March as we sat on our living room balcony.

"It's up to him. He hasn't mentioned Fisnik for weeks and I'm not going to pressure him."

"What do you talk about at the bar now?"

"Hmm, this and that," I said, though to tell the truth, Fisnik being a taboo subject had left a big vacuum in our conversations and we often stood up at the bar gabbing with the other blokes.

"It's my birthday a fortnight today, Ken."

"I know, dear," I said, though I'd forgotten, again.

"Hmm, I bet you don't even remember how old I am."

"Sixty-three," I said, quick as a flash.

"No, I'll be sixty-four."

"Sixty-three now, I meant," as I knew it was one or the other.

"When I used to listen to that Beatles song, I always thought I'd like to do something special for my sixty-fourth, assuming I was still alive."

"Well, you're very much alive and you've just got back from that trip to Gibraltar. Wasn't that special enough?"

"No, it was not. All we did was drive there, shop, eat English food, and drive back."

"You saw the monkeys, didn't you?"

"Yes, one stole Harvey's sandwich. That was the high spot of the trip. Do you know what I'd really like for my birthday, Ken?"

"Go on," I said, steeling myself.

"It's two things, really."

"To eat cake and drink cava?"

"Ha, no, well that as well. What I'd like is one of those dinky little video cameras and... well..."

"Go on, the suspense is killing me."

"I'd like Fisnik to do another exhibition and for you to film me when I buy a picture and he does his little routine," she said, too quickly for me to interrupt.

"You can have the video camera," I said. "The cash from the first and *only* exhibition will pay for that."

"Aw, Ken."

"Doreen, if it was up to me we'd be doing shows at least once a fortnight, but it's down to Fede and he's not up for it."

"Can you not drop a hint? It's been two months since the last one. Has he been painting?"

"I think so."

"Well then? I thought you said his wife wanted the house habitable before the summer. You could mention that."

"Hmm, I've *thought* about saying to him that if he signed a few pictures with his Fisnik signature, I could try to flog them for him."

"Well, you might sell a few, but it's the performance that everyone wants to see, and if he leaves it any longer people might lose interest. Does he not need the money? That could be a big incentive."

"He never mentions it, though he did say that his car's on its last legs."

"I know!" she cried, grabbing my leg.

"Get off. You frightened me to death."

"Sell him our car."

"What's the point in that? It's just a car."

"Sell it him cheap. Tell him… tell him…" She grasped her forehead and I thought steam was about to pour out of her ears. "How much is it worth?"

"I don't know. About five thousand now, I guess, or a bit less."

"Tell him you'll sell it him for four, but that he has to be quick as you've got another one lined up." She leant back in her wicker chair, exhausted by the effort.

"I like my car," I said, though I did fancy one of those four by fours that are a bit easier to get into, me being an old codger. "And it'd be a blooming expensive incentive for us."

"At least say something to him when you see him. Mention my birthday, or the car, or both, but just see if he'll do it, *please*, Ken."

"I'll say something tomorrow night, but don't get your hopes up.

"Thanks, Ken."

I lit my pipe.

"I know you'll be able to persuade him."

"I'm trying to think."

"Sorry, Ken," she said, before wisely leaving me alone with my deliberations. Heck, I was just as keen as Doreen to get the Fisnik show back on the road.

# 12

Yes, I too thought it was about time I dropped a few hints to Fede about resurrecting Fisnik, but it was Doreen's birthday request that inspired me to act the very next evening, but in my own way, of course.

"How's that car of yours?" I asked him after leading him over to a table, having told him that my left knee was playing up.

"Knackered. I've been taking the bus into Málaga and I daren't even risk driving to the house last Sunday," he said, looking downcast.

"So no painting then?"

"No, and I hate staying in the flat. I'll have to get a new car."

"I was thinking of selling mine and getting one of those all-terrain vehicles, second hand, of course."

"Really?"

"Yes, I've been thinking about it for a while. They're easier to get in and out of," I said, rubbing my perfectly sound knee.

"It's a nice car yours. How much are you selling it for?"

"Oh, I've been told I'll get at least €4,500 for it, but I'd take four if I could sell it quick. There's a nice second-hand Nissan at a garage on the main road, but someone'll buy it soon, no doubt."

"I could see about a loan, I suppose," he said, sipping his beer pensively.

"Hmm, shame to pay interest though. Listen, if you could manage to pay me half soon, I could let you have the car and you could pay me the rest over the next few months."

"But you have to buy the other car."

"I can manage that with two thousand from you," I said. The truth was that I could have bought a brand new one if I'd wanted to, but I'm a tight-fisted old sod really, and it was all about dangling this Fisnik-inducing carrot. "What do you think? It's a great car. Pedro really looked after it and I've just had it serviced."

"It's a good idea, but I'm a bit skint at the moment. I've just bought a load of new paints, brushes and canvases and it'll take me a while to raise the money."

"So you're painting as much as ever?"

"Yes, and you'll laugh at this, but I'm still doing a lot of Albanian paintings, mainly of those churches."

"That's the Fisnik in you," I said with a laugh. "Another beer?"

"My turn," he said, and went to the bar.

As he waited to be served I observed him out of the corner of my eye. He was moving from one foot to the other and I hoped that his mind had become as restless as his legs. When he returned with the bottles and a plate of olives I was engrossed in the football match.

"That Messi's a marvel, isn't he?" I said absently.

"Yes, he is." He looked at me. "Ken?"

"Yes?"

"All this about the car – your very kind offer, I mean – it's not all a ruse to get me to do another exhibition, is it?"

"What? Of course not. We haven't talked about that for weeks, have we?"

"No, but… I don't know. Do you know what I'd really like to do, Ken?"

"What?" I asked, tapping my chair leg.

"I'd like to exhibit my paintings, but as me, Federico Pérez Martín."

"I suppose you *could* do that," I said, scratching my chin and looking a bit doubtful, before deciding to take the longer route round to my objective. "Yes, I mean, why not? It's the paintings that count and the Fisnik business could never last." I became more enthusiastic. "I bet we could get the restaurant in the village again. Juan would arrange that. Shall I ask him?"

"Well, I'll need to think about it first," he said, swirling the beer in his bottle and studying it.

"Just give me the word and I'll speak to him." I looked over at the telly. "Two-one to Barcelona."

I became engrossed in the game for a while, but I could see that Fede had become very fidgety. I bided my time.

"Perhaps you could call him now," he finally said.

"Who?"

"Juan."

"Hmm, he might be busy, but I suppose I could try him," I said, ever so glad that Doreen had insisted that I take the mobile phone with me.

I fiddled about with it for a bit before calling our landline.

"Hello," said my wife, which showed how many Spanish friends *she* had.

"Hola, Juan, can you speak now?"

"Is that you, Ken."

"Great, it's just that I'm with Fede and he's thinking about doing another exhibition, not as Fisnik, but as himself."

"It's me, Ken. Doreen."

"Yes, like he says, it's better to be himself if he wants to get a reputation in the long run."

"Ah, I see what you're up to, I think," she said.

"Yes... right... good idea. So you'll speak to the owner tomorrow? Thanks, Juan, I'll call you in the afternoon."

"But I want him to be Fisnik. Tell him that, Ken. It's no—"

"OK, Juan, hasta mañana." I hung up, cutting off Doreen in full flow. "He'll speak to the owner tomorrow."

"Great," Fede said, looking his old self again. "I've got lots of new paintings. They're mostly smaller ones, so they ought to sell."

"Yes, though it's a shame you won't be able to sell the Albanian ones."

"Hmm, I hadn't thought of that."

"I'm just nipping out for a smoke."

After a leisurely smoke I returned inside. I saw that Fede was spinning his empty bottle between his palms, so I ordered two more.

"What if I just tell everyone at the exhibition that I was Fisnik, or Fisnik was me, and that it was just a stunt? Then I could exhibit my Albanian paintings too."

"Oh, I don't know." I grimaced and moved my head from side to side. "I know these guiris and they might not take kindly to that. Some of them might even want their money back."

"Oh."

"Fisnik made a real hit, you see, and seeing plain old Fede might be a big disappointment to them. You know, no costume, no chanting, no foot kissing. People are still talking about it even now."

"I won't be Fisnik again," he said, eyeing me a bit suspiciously.

"Fair enough. I'll speak to Juan tomorrow."

"Thanks. I'll call you in the evening."

About twenty-two hours later I was in the flat when the phone rang.

"I'll get it, Doreen. It'll be Fede."

I'd filled her in about my crafty plan and she smiled encouragingly as I walked into my little room. I won't bore you with another whole conversation, but I told Fede straight off that Juan was pessimistic about any non-Fisnik exhibition plans up in the village. Like me, he was worried that the punters might turn nasty when they saw that Fisnik was just a tubby little Spanish chap, and he wasn't prepared to risk displeasing the restaurant owner, in case he ever wanted to work there again. This wasn't a complete fabrication, as I had spoken to Juan, but it was me who had put those thoughts into his head.

"So we'll have to look for somewhere else to do your exhibition," I told Fede.

"Well, as myself I'm happy to do one here in town. Maybe the restaurant where Juan works now would let us use it on a Monday when they close."

"I already thought of that. I asked Juan to ask his boss and he said no." This wasn't true, but I had to improvise.

"No?"

"No, his boss said that he'd done a few in the past and they were flops, apart from one African chap who drew quite a crowd with some carvings," I said, finding it far easier to fib on the phone than face-to-face, but I stopped myself before I got carried away.

"Oh," was all he said.

"I spoke to Pedro too and he suggested a place called Frigiliana."

"I know it. A pretty place with lots of arty shops."

"If you like, I could ask him to call a few places and see if they might be interested, or you could do it yourself."

This was a calculated risk, but if they did accept Fede as Fede, all the better for him. I could always ask him to dress up and do his act one day just for Doreen, though it wouldn't be quite the same.

"Yes, I'm off work tomorrow, so I'll look up the numbers and ring a few."

"You do that, Fede."

"Are you busy this weekend?"

"Not especially. Why?"

"Well, I was wondering if you could run me over to the house one day. My car's had it and I'm dying to do some painting."

"No problem. Saturday's good for me."

"You'd have to pick me up later though."

"No need. I'll go off for a walk and then we'll have lunch and then I'll read in the sun for a bit," I said, more than happy to enjoy the country air while I watched Fisnik coming slowly back to life. "I'll pick you up at nine."

"Thanks. Hopefully I'll have some good news about Frigiliana by then."

"I hope so."


"Well?" asked Doreen when I emerged from my den.

I brought her up to date.

"So you think you might persuade him on Saturday?" she asked.

"No."

"No?"

"No, but I hope to see him persuade himself."

"You're a clever one, Ken. I'd better order my video camera then, so it'll be here for my birthday."

"You do that," I said, tapping her playfully on the head for luck.

# 13

When Fede left his block of flats and approached the car on Saturday morning he looked every bit as glum as I'd expected him to. From what I'd heard, Frigiliana appeared to be chock-a-block with potters and artists, so why on earth would they want to exhibit an unknown local painter?

"Buenos días, Fede," I said cheerfully.

"Hola, Ken," he said, less cheerfully.

"Did you get out of bed on the wrong side this morning?"

"What?"

"I mean, you don't look very happy."

"We say 'to get up on the left foot' here," he said.

"Oh well, that's something new I've learnt then. My Spanish is still bad."

"Not as bad as my painting, it appears," he said, stamping on a few passing ants, not like Fede at all.

"Why do you say that?"

"I went up to Frigiliana yesterday. I thought it'd be better than phoning. I took a couple of small paintings with me and showed them round the shops and restaurants."

"And?"

"They weren't interested in doing an exhibition."

"But did they say your paintings were no good?" I asked. I was surprised, though I still didn't really have a clue if they *were* any good.

"No, in fact most people liked them, but they said that I'd have to get better known before they'd let me exhibit."

"I guess that's always the way," I said, looking suitably glum, but rejoicing inside. That sounds selfish, but I just knew that the Fisnik touch would make all the difference.

You only have to look at the famous artists these days to see that half the battle is getting noticed, and if they have to cut a cow in half to do it, that's what they do, the daft pillocks. Being Fisnik was an innocent gimmick compared to some of the stuff that goes on in that world of charlatans.

"Your pictures are definitely good," I said as we drove towards the house, my confidence in his ability restored.

"I know, but I've realised how hard it is to sell them."

"Hmm," was all I said just then.

When we got to the house Fede unlocked the door and fell upon his art stuff like a man possessed, not having painted for almost a fortnight. Despite his involuntary break, there were at least as many paintings around the place as on my first visit. After making some coffee and taking him a cup, I sat outside in the warming sun to drink mine, before heading off up a rough track into the hills.

After about half an hour I was starting to get out of puff, so I sat down on a rock to admire the views of the mountains, village and plastic greenhouses, before ambling back to the house. At about two I managed to lure him away from a small canvas that I forgot to look at, with the promise of a slap-up lunch in the village.

Wine mellows a man, as most of us know, and after we'd polished off our fried sardines and bull's tail stew, washed down by a couple of bottles of heady red wine, we were both feeling as mellow as could be.

"Ah, it feels good to be painting again, Ken," said Fede, patting his paunch.

"Borrow the car tomorrow, if you like. I'm not using it."

"Are you sure?"

"Yes."

"Thanks, Ken. I think I'd have stayed overnight otherwise. Ah, I love painting."

"Have you thought about what I said about the car, about buying it, I mean?"

"Yes, I've thought about it."

"I really need to sell it in the next week or two. I've set my heart on that Nissan."

"Well, I'm pretty sure that I can get at least half of the money within a fortnight, or three weeks at the most, so you could go ahead and pay them a deposit so they'll keep it for you."

"Right," I said, fearing that he'd found another way to raise the cash. "I'll do that then," I added, resolving to go and look for a Nissan four-by-four on Monday.

Fede seemed to be amused about something, so I felt disinclined to bring the subject round to paintings – and the selling of them – until I knew what he was up to.

On the way back to the house he became positively giddy and I hoped he hadn't overdone it with the grape juice, though he'd drunk no more than a bottle of it.

"Come and look at this watercolour I'm painting, Ken," he said with a chortle as he unlocked the door.

I walked round the easel and what I saw elated me more than half a gallon of wine could have.

"Bloody hell, does this mean...?"

"Yes, Ken, you've convinced me with your subtle ways, but it'll be his last ever appearance, so we'd better make it count."

"We can make some copies of that for a start," I said, looking at an amazingly clear and non-abstract likeness of Fisnik, dressed in black from head to pointed toes, with cap, glasses, cape and all.

"That's why I've painted it. I just have to add where and when the exhibition will take place, and then do some copies for posters."

"You could knock me down with a feather," I said, neither knowing nor caring if folk said it in Spanish, as its meaning was clear enough. "When did you decide you'd do it?"

"Well, offering to sell me your car planted a seed, though my trip to Frigiliana settled the matter. I knew it was a long shot, because this coast is plagued with painters, but I decided to go anyway."

"Do you think they'd like Fisnik there?"

"You know, I think they would, but I'd rather use the same place as last time, if Juan can arrange it. We need to do it soon, so it's our best option."

"Can I confess something to you, Fede?"

"Let me guess."

"Go on."

"That you had no intention of buying a new car."

"Yes."

"Yes, you had?"

"No, yes, I hadn't."

"Ha, I knew it. You're a good friend, Ken."

"Still, it got me thinking and I do fancy a change now, so the offer still stands, though if you give me a thousand you can have it and pay me the rest bit by bit. We're not badly off, really, and a nice second-hand all-terrain car will be just right for carting Fisnik's paintings around."

"I'm only doing one more show, Ken. I'm adamant about that," he said, doing his best to look adamant.

"I know, and I think you're right, but that's no reason for us not to carry on selling his works afterwards."

"It'd be risky for me to do that. I do look a *bit* like him, after all," he said, glancing at the picture.

"Not for me and Doreen though, and it'll get us out and about. Pedro and Juan will help too. Shall I ring Juan? He's probably resting now."

"Yes, ring him."

I rang Juan and he called back ten minutes later with the news that Fisnik's last ever exhibition would take place a week on Tuesday at the same restaurant in the village, which just happened – and this is true – to be Doreen's sixty-fourth birthday.

"Shall we rehearse?" I asked Fede when I'd switched off the phone.

"Next Sunday will be soon enough. Fisnik's only hiding beneath the surface, after all. I'll go and finish off our poster."

"Attaboy."

"What?"

"Good lad."

I often seem to finish off chapters by reporting back to Doreen, but she was the last person I saw every day, and she was usually thirsting for news.

"Well?"

"Well what?"

"What happened?" she asked.

"Nothing much. We went to his house, he painted a picture, and I pottered about."

"Nothing else?"

"We had lunch in the village," I said, striving to keep a straight face.

"What about Fisnik?"

"What about him?"

"Will Fede appear as him again, or not?"

"I'm not sure, but there's a glimmer of hope," I said, retreating behind the settee in case she started pawing me.

"Really? Do tell me, Ken," she said, her brown eyes wide with anticipation.

"Well, he dropped one tiny hint."

"What was that?" she said, beginning to pursue me.

"Oh, it was something in the picture that he painted."

"What?" she asked as we began to circle the settee.

"A subtle clue."

"What clue?"

"Well, it was a watercolour of Fisnik."

"Oh, Ken! Surely that means he'll appear again."

"Hmm, maybe. He did write something on the picture too," I said as I began my second lap of the sofa.

"What, Ken? What?"

"Oh, just the place and date of his next and last exhibition, to make posters out of it."

"Oh, Ken!" she said, backing me into a corner and hugging me.

"Get off," I said, patting her on the back.

"When's it to be?"

I would have loved to have teased her about that too. Most couples have their funny way and one of ours was for me to tease her mercilessly, but I had to tell her the details as I'd be counting on her to spread the word to the expat contingent.

"It'll be at the same place."

"When?"

"I've forgotten," I said, backing away towards the bathroom.

"*Please* tell me, Ken."

I stepped into the bathroom. "On your birthday," I said, before deftly locking the door.

Doreen whooped for joy, bless her.

# 14

The following week was a busy one, as there was much to be done if Fisnik's swansong were to be the success that I anticipated. I mean, I was happy for Fede to pay for the car in instalments, but if he could settle up from his huge takings, all the better.

As he was working all week, he brought me the precious poster picture when he returned my car keys the following evening.

"Is it not a bit big to copy," I asked him as we supped a quick beer.

"No, it's just A3 size, so any photocopying place will do it."

I waved away the twenty euro note that he proffered. "Are you going to do the same routine as last time?" I asked him.

"I think so, don't you?"

"I guess so, but a final flourish would be good."

"Like what?" he asked.

"Maybe something that'll make it clear that you'll not be appearing ever again."

"A mock suicide?"

"Er, no, I don't think so, though it'd be great for posthumous sales. I'll have a think about it."

"Me too. Thanks, Ken."

"Thank *you*, Fede, for bringing Fisnik back to life. Doreen's delighted. It'll be her best birthday since the one when I finally agreed to marry her."

"Ha, Fisnik will think of something special for her."

Never one to do things by halves, or hardly ever, I printed a hundred copies of the poster, thanked them for sticking one up in the shop window, and set about distributing the other ninety-nine.

Juan was kind enough to spend his day off plastering Fuentecastillo with them, and Pedro took care of the village, while Doreen and I hit the road to spread the word further afield, driving as far as Nerja and Frigiliana to the east, though I drew the line at going as far as Malaga to the west.

"There might be a few Albanians around, and the poster says Fisnik's from there, so it's too risky," I said to Doreen as we headed into the hills to tour the numerous, expat-infested villages.

On Tuesday evening I met Fede for a beer and handed over my car keys.

"In case you want to go and paint a bit more," I said.

"Thanks, I will, but I've got about thirty pictures to sell."

"We might need a few more small ones," I said, before naming all the places we'd visited.

"Bloody hell," he said, which were the only English words he'd picked up off me. "I'll do a few more Albanian ones."

"Pick me up at nine on Sunday and I'll come with you," I said. "Then we can finalise the details. Are you nervous about it?"

"Not as much as last time. I might even enjoy it, because who knows when I'll get another chance to play the clown?"

"That's the spirit."

On Wednesday I thought I'd better find myself a new car, as I planned to hand mine over to Fede after Fisnik had said his final farewell. I strolled out of town to a biggish dealer's and, after a quick test drive, paid a deposit on a green Hyundai four-by-four which only cost me a couple of grand more than the car I was selling.

"I'll pick it up a week today," I said to the sycophantic, guiri-loving salesman. "I'll probably be paying most of it in cash. Is that all right?"

"Oh, yes," he said, as they're fond of cash deals in Spain, being even less inclined to pay taxes than us Brits.

That's how optimistic I was about the exhibition, you see, as the expats had been informed that it would be the last one and many seemed likely to invest in fine Albanian artwork while they could. We'd also decided to lower the prices of the small Albanian pictures – almost all of domed churches – by about half, in order to shift a few more.

"You'd better open this now," I said to Doreen on Monday morning, giving her the box containing the dinky video camera which she'd handed over to me for wrapping.

"Ooh, I wonder what it is," she said.

"Ha, you'd better learn how to use it, and then show me."

"Thanks, Ken, it's just what I wanted," she said after tearing off the brown paper wrapping. "You were late back from Fede's yesterday. Have you planned anything new?"

"No, it'll be just the same as last time, except we'll sell more."

"I'm sure, but I bet you've got something up your sleeves."

"Ah-ha!" I said, before retiring to the balcony to smoke my pipe.

# 15

"All set?" I asked Fede when he picked me up at eight, my car being practically his already.

"Yes, I did two more paintings last night. I feel like a bit of a fraud."

"Why?"

"Well, doing the paintings so quickly. It's easy to do new versions of existing ones, but it seems a lot to ask €200 for something I've done in a couple of hours. I'm not even sure if they'll be completely dry yet."

"People have painted canvases in just one colour and sold them for millions. At least there's a church or something in yours."

"I suppose so."

I don't like repeating myself, so I'll just tell you that until eleven o'clock things went much the same as during our previous exhibition. Juan and Pedro cleared the restaurant and set up the pictures, I kept popping out to the car to reassure Fisnik that it would all go well, and no-one walked through the door until an hour after we'd opened.

Doreen arrived first, with all her friends and acquaintances, including quite a few people who hadn't attended last time. Juan despatched a score of drinks at lightning speed, but the Fuentecastillo expats' arrival proved to be the calm before the storm. As more and more people trooped in, I decided it was time to summon the main attraction.

Fisnik must have thought the time was right too, as no sooner had I stepped outside than I saw him shuffling towards me. Unlike the nervous wreck I'd witnessed on his first ever appearance, however, I beheld a beaming artist all set to knock them dead.

Rather than the polite murmuring he'd provoked the first time, he was greeted by a round of applause, which he acknowledged by bowing deeply, not once, but several times, saying 'Bienvenidos, welcome, mirëpritur!' after each bow. By the time he reached his chair in the corner, I had his small glass of brandy ready, so he faced the throng, raised his glass, and cried, 'Salud, cheers, gëzuar!'

This trilingual business, which had been a joint idea of Fede and me, went down a treat and as soon as the maestro sat down and assumed a solemn, almost mystical, expression, people began to appropriate paintings. Having anticipated this eventuality – in my optimistic moments, at least – I rounded up the discerning purchasers and led them over to a window not far from where Fisnik was sitting.

When there were six of them, comprising Doreen's friend Mildred, four other Brits who I knew by sight, and a Scandinavian-looking young lady, I announced the first part of the master plan which Fede and I had dreamt up two days earlier.

"Everybody who buys a picture gets free drinks for the rest of the day," I said to the little group in English. "Within reason," I added, as one red-faced chap's eyes lit up more than I'd have liked. "Now we have to wait for two more buyers," I said.

"Why's that?" said the red-faced chap, keen to get back to the bar.

"Because out of every eight people, one will get their painting free."

This revelation caused rather more gleeful anticipation than the free booze incentive.

"How will he decide?" asked the blonde lady.

"You'll see. It's his last ever exhibition in Spain, as he's been given permission to return to his homeland, so he wants to make this gesture before he leaves. Feel free to chat to your friends until we're ready. I'll look after your paintings."

As expected, they all hurried off into the crowd to spread the news about the one-in-eight chance of getting a freebie, so within a couple of minutes two more people had grabbed a picture and joined me by the window.

"Make way, ladies and gentlemen, please," I said as I led them all over to Fisnik's domain. As I lined them up with their paintings, the chattering died down, and when silence had fallen the maestro rose from his chair and slowly stretched out his arms, to get that overgrown crow effect, before raising them into the air.

"Every man is the smith of his own fortune," he cried, before repeating the very apt phrase in Spanish and Albanian.

He lowered his arms and nodded to me, before turning slowly round to face the wall.

"You must all change places and form a semi-circle now," I told them, before whipping a black cloth out of my pocket with a flourish. After blindfolding Fisnik I turned him round and led him to a point just in front of them.

"Now Fisnik's assistants will look after your paintings while you hold hands and form a circle around the maestro," I said dramatically, having got into the swing of things by then.

Pedro and Juan came over to collect the pictures and the circle was soon complete.

"When you are ready, Maestro Fisnik," I said slowly in Spanish.

He gave a little bow, before beginning to spin around slowly, chanting the following well-rehearsed mantra:

"Fisnik of Albania wishes you health and fortune! Fisnik de Albania os desea salud y fortuna! Fisnik e Shqipërisë dëshiron ju shëndet dhe pasuri!"

(Doreen looked up the Albanian, by the way.)

On uttering the final word he came to a halt, stepped forward slowly with his arms outstretched, and embraced the person he touched. It was a close thing between Mildred and the red-faced man, and Fede told me later that the smell of wine on his breath had made him adjust his line ever so slightly, so it was Doreen's friend who got her picture free, while the red-faced man spent the next two hours drowning his sorrows, before his wife helped him out to their car.

So, after I'd removed Fisnik's blindfold and adjusted his dark glasses, Mildred was the first to get her feet kissed, followed by the others in the order in which they produced the cash. Once the rather hesitant lush had coughed up and had his sandals kissed, Fisnik jumped to his feet and, as three of the pictures had been Albanian ones, he rushed out crying, 'Albania, Shqipëri, Albania, Shqipëri!' just like last time.

"That was good," said Doreen when she approached me at the bar where I was quaffing a well-earned caña. "A bit over the top, though."

"Well, it's the last time, so we've pulled out all the stops," I said under my breath.

"Shall I get into the next group of eight with my picture?"

"No, you'll be the last one to get the treatment and your painting's been chosen and stowed away."

"Has it? I can't wait. Look, there are four people waiting with their pictures already."

"Right, could you go and give Fisnik a shout?" I said, before weaving my way through the crowd to the discerning buyers. Well, discerning or fond of a flutter, I thought at the time.

"A word in your ear, Ken," said Harvey as I tried to squeeze past him unnoticed.

"Not now, Harvey, I'm busy," I said, but he put his hand on my arm.

"*I* think I've *seen* Fisnik somewhere," he whispered in my ear."

"Have you been out walking in the country?" I asked, though it was unlikely that he'd stray more than a few hundred yards from a bar.

"No, we went to Seville last week."

"Ah, that's nice. We haven't been there yet."

"We went on the bus."

"Easier than driving there, I guess."

"The driver looked very much like Fisnik."

"Well, you know, he is European, after all. There are plenty of Spaniards who look a bit like him," I said, hiding a big gulp with my hand.

"That man looked a *lot* like him, Ken," he said, his subsequent leer suggesting that he wasn't making this revelation just for the fun of it.

"Well, you're mistaken, that's all," I said, thinking of the swift punch to the solar plexus that I might have given him in my younger days.

"I might just go and ask him if he remembers me from the bus trip."

"I wouldn't do that, Harvey," I said with the tiniest hint of menace.

"Ha."

"It might put him off and spoil the show for everyone," I said, appealing to his better nature.

"Hum."

"He's very sensitive," I said, clutching at straws.

"Humph."

"What do you want, Harvey?"

"Nothing," he said, his leer starting to look more like a smile.

"Do you want a painting?"

"No, I've got one, and it looks just fine in our hallway."

"Well..." I began, glancing over at the growing group of punters waiting for an audience with Fisnik, and feeling thoroughly stumped.

"There is one little thing that I'd like, Ken."

"Go on."

"Well, this is the last show, isn't it?"

"The last exhibition, yes."

"But *we* know that the supposed Albanian isn't going back to his supposed country, don't we?"

"If you say so, Harvey."

"But there's nothing to stop him selling more paintings after he's gone back," he said, lifting his fingers to apostrophise the last two words.

"I guess not."

"I want to be his agent, or one of them. I want to handle some of his paintings and take a ten percent cut. Can you arrange that, Ken?"

"We'll see how you behave for the rest of the day, Harvey."

"I want at least a dozen good-sized paintings to sell. I'll tell you why later. You'll be surprised. Word of honour?"

"OK."

He held out his hand.

I shook it and made my way over to the awaiting buyers, a bit rattled to say the least.

There were already nine people standing by the window with their chosen masterpieces, so I asked our old neighbour Shirley to wait for the next batch, before leading the eager group over to Fisnik. I was in such a state of shock at that point that it took me half a minute to register that the stingy Shirley was actually splashing out on a painting. I looked over and saw that hers was just a €100 one, so maybe she was a cautious speculator, or a closet gambler.

The ensuing ritual took my mind off Harvey for a while. After I'd watched Fisnik make his vociferous exit and congratulated a local man on his free painting, my heartbeat went back down to somewhere near normal. It clearly wasn't in Harvey's interests to sabotage the exhibition, and it was up to Fede to decide whether to let him sell pictures or tell him to sod off. I put the slimy scoundrel out of my mind, knocked back the caña that Juan had slid over to me, went to relieve myself, and joined the growing group by the window.

By the time two more groups had experienced the Fisnik phenomenon, the great man was looking fatigued and sounding hoarse. The crowd had thinned and there were only five paintings left, mostly larger ones, so I decided it was time to wind up proceedings.

I wanted Doreen to be the last person to receive her picture, but I didn't want the place to be empty when she did, so by means of a little guesswork and a few polite enquiries I ascertained that the fifteen or so stragglers were there for the ambience, the wine, or both, so I told Fisnik that the time was ripe for his last ever performance.

"I'm ready, Ken," he said with a tired smile.

I too mustered up my remaining energy and clapped my hands.

"Ladies and gentlemen, damas y caballeros. The last act of the day, el último acto del día," I boomed. "Mrs Doreen Tonks, step this way, please."

She made her way towards me, thrilled at being the centre of attention. She handed me the video camera, which I passed to Juan, and all except Pedro gathered round. As most of the remaining folk were either British or other foreigners, I made my little speech just in English.

"Doreen, on this, the occasion of your sixty-fourth birthday, I would like to present you with a special painting done by Fisnik especially for you."

During the polite applause a little ruse occurred to me which I thought might make the dastardly Harvey regret his avaricious plotting.

"Harvey, would you be so kind as to unveil this masterful work of art."

I thought he'd look suitably sheepish, but not a bit of it. He strode over, took the painting from my hands, and deftly stripped it of its colourful wrapping.

Fede hadn't allowed me to see it, and nor had Fisnik, but there we were, Doreen and me, posing together in front of an orthodox church. It was no more abstract than the painting that he'd done of himself as Fisnik, and the fact that he'd had only one photograph of us to work from made it all the more remarkable. Maybe I'm biased because he made us look a bit younger and slimmer than we were, but it was universally admired, before Harvey handed it to me and I presented it to my wife, the camera whirring all the while.

Then Fisnik approached and stretched his arms out wide.

"Happy birthday! Feliz cumpleaños! Gëzuar ditëlindjen!" he cried hoarsely as he raised his hands, before falling slowly to his knees and kissing a pair of shoes for the last time in his life.

He stood up slowly and bowed, first to Doreen, and then to the company at large, before walking towards the door. A hush had fallen and before he slipped out of sight he turned to face us.

"Goodbye forever! Adiós para siempre! Lamtumirë përgjithmonë!" he said, before smiling, swishing his cape, and leaving.

I assumed a perturbed look and spoke up before the chattering began. "Will he have gone to the car, do you think?" I asked Juan in Spanish.

"I don't know," he replied with a worried look, and we both hurried to the door, followed by practically everybody else.

The wide pavement outside overlooked a narrow street which led to an unpaved track that headed downhill into the countryside. By the time we were all assembled, Fisnik was to be seen shuffling rapidly along the track before disappearing from view around a tree-lined bend.

"Where do you think he's gone?" asked Janet, wife of the perfidious Harvey.

"Down to his shack, I suppose, before heading back to Albania," I said clearly, wishing that someone else had asked, as I reasoned that she must be privy to her husband's underhand antics.

"Such a shame that we'll not see him again," she said with such convincing sincerity that I thought maybe she hadn't noticed Fede on the bus.

"A great pity. Such a talented artist," said Harvey with equal candour, leaving me none the wiser.

"That's all folks. Let's just hope he sends us some paintings from his homeland," I said, meeting Harvey's placid eyes, the rascal.

We trooped back inside. I said goodbye to the faithful, gave Doreen a quick kiss, it being her birthday, and Juan and I saw them out and locked the door.

"A great success," he said.

"Yes, it was," I replied, deciding not to dampen things by mentioning Harvey's foul play.

"A beer?"

"Please, Juan, in one of the pint glasses that the guiris use."

# 16

I had polished off the pint and made inroads into another when we heard a knock on the door.

"Welcome back," I said to Fede, who had changed into his normal clothes. "Where's Pedro?"

"He's gone to park your car."

"Your car now, Fede. I'll pick mine up tomorrow. A brandy?"

"No, that's Fisnik's drink. Just a caña, please."

By the time Pedro returned – he'd been waiting for Fisnik further along the track, of course – Fede had turned out his pockets and I'd counted the takings.

"I make it €4,620."

"Fantastic," said Juan.

"Marvellous," said Pedro.

"May Fisnik enjoy life back in Albania," I said.

"Fisnik has been good to us," said Fede, before counting out a pile of notes and pocketing them. "I need to take three thousand, as I have a car to pay for," he said, almost apologetically.

"At least," I said, though I thought it was about right, as Juan, Pedro and myself had all worked hard.

I came out of it with six hundred, plus three thousand down on the car, which was fine by me, and once that business was taken care of – money's always a slightly sordid subject, however you make it – we relaxed, ate, and drank some more, especially me, as Fede would be driving me home.

"Is Fisnik dead and buried now, Fede, or might he paint a few more pictures?" I asked a while later.

"Well, I want to get back do doing more creative work," he said. "Art isn't all about making money."

"Of course not," said Juan, looking a bit doubtful. Juan was still living with his cousin, you see, and would have moved heaven and earth to make enough money to rent a place of his own.

"*But*, I also want to continue working on the Albanian churches, and maybe mosques too, and Fisnik will have to sign those, I think."

"Maybe we could take a trip there some day, so you can get some inspiration," I said.

"Yes, I'd like that a lot," Fede said, as I'd hoped he would.

"Perhaps you could sell some of Fisnik's new work to raise some cash for the trip," I said.

"Maybe. One thing I do know for sure."

"What's that, Fede?"

"That my wife wants most of her little house back before the summer, so I'll have to try to sell most of what I paint from now on, whether they're my work or Fisnik's."

"We could help you to sell Fisnik's pictures," said Juan.

"I'm sure I'd sell a few up here in the village," said Pedro.

"I'll leave that to you two, then," I said, happy to draw a line under my foray into the art world. Both Juan and Pedro needed the cash much more than me, after all. "There is one thing I ought to mention, though."

"What's that?" asked Fede.

"Well, you know Harvey?"

"The English drunk?"

"Yes, he told me that he'd spotted you driving the bus to Seville."

"Really?"

"Yes, and he sort of threatened to expose you, until he extracted a promise from me."

"A promise?"

"Yes, he wants to help to sell Fisnik's painting's too, and take a ten percent commission."

"Tell him to go to hell," he said.

"I will. He said he had a good reason for doing it, but that's no way to go about things."

"I wonder what his reason is," said Juan, maybe fearing that Harvey might scupper his little sideline.

Just then there was a knock on the door.

"That'll be the owner," said Juan, standing up.

We heard words exchanged outside, before Juan returned. "It's that guiri you just mentioned, Ken. He wants a word with you."

"Tell him to go and fry asparagus, Ken," said Fede, that being another way of saying go to hell.

I stepped outside and found Harvey sitting on a bench, with Janet beside him.

"Well?" I asked, looking only at the skunk in human form.

"Ken, I want to explain the reasons behind my… er, strange actions this morning."

"I'm shocked at what he's done, Ken," said Janet. "I wanted him to suggest the idea, but not like that."

"I was feeling… well, mischievous. That's why I teased you a bit."

"A bit? I nearly had a heart attack, you bastard," I said. "Sorry, Janet," I added, the uncouth youth inside me having popped out for a minute.

"It's like this, Ken. I asked Harvey to ask you to ask Fisnik, or whatever his real name is, to let us sell a few of his pictures to raise money for the animal sanctuary. I wish I'd asked you myself now," she said, staring daggers at her cowering husband.

"Sorry, Ken, I got a bit carried away. Wine on an empty stomach, you know. Thought I was back at boarding school for a minute."

"Well, I think you've messed it up now. I just mentioned it to Fede and he's not impressed."

"I told you, you imbecile!" Janet said to her wilting spouse.

"I'll see what I can do, but it's not looking good."

"Thanks, Ken. Sorry, Ken," said the contrite one.

"You will be by the time I've finished with you. Come on. Bye, Ken, and sorry," she said, showing a new, fearsome side to her character. Harvey was in for it, and I was glad.

I locked the door, Juan poured me another beer, and I filled them in on my little exchange.

"He can still go to the devil," said Fede. "What's this English obsession with animals all about, anyway?"

"Well, they, I mean we, like them, I suppose. At the sanctuary they take in donkeys that have been mistreated, dogs that have been abandoned, and other animals in distress," I said, hinting that if some Spaniards weren't so cruel to our dumb chums there'd be no need for us foreigners to rescue them.

Maybe Fede had once kicked a dog, or perhaps it was simply the fact that he was a good bloke, but I could see that he was relenting.

"Juan and Pedro are going to be the only people to sell Fisnik's paintings," he said, making Juan's lips curl up ever so slightly. "But I might, or might not, let the Englishman try to sell the works of Federico Pérez Martín. I'll think about it."

"I'll tell him that when I see him, that you'll think about it. Let's keep him guessing for a while."

"The trouble with some of these guiris is that they drink too much," said Fede, shaking his head.

"Anything else before I clean up?" asked Juan.

We all had one more drink.

*   *   *

"I still smile when I think about my birthday, Ken," Doreen said a few weeks later.

"Yes, it was quite an event. I doubt you'll have any more that are so exciting."

We were sitting on a café terrace down by the sea, enjoying the warm evening breeze. Things had panned out quite nicely since Fisnik's return to Albania and I often popped over to see Fede in the country. He was painting away as much as ever, and no sooner had he finished a picture than it was despatched to Juan, Pedro or Harvey for them to find a buyer.

Fisnik's churches and mosques were selling like hot cakes, and Fede's new line of commercial art had also found a market, much to Harvey and Janet's delight, and the animals' benefit. Doreen and me had a hand in that, because Fede's painting of us had provoked a few enquiries, so, after I'd got the go-ahead from the artist, Doreen made some colour photocopies and told folk that he'd be happy to paint them and their loved ones for a modest, but not too modest, fee. We let the slightly less dissipated Harvey handle those too.

It wasn't too long before a lot of the Brits knew that Fisnik was really Fede, but that just made things more interesting, because those who were in the know enjoyed spreading the Albanian myth to those who weren't, and as gossip seems to make the expat world go round, I think there's still quite a bit of mileage left in our little hoax.

"Shall we have a drive over to the animal sanctuary tomorrow, Ken?" Doreen asked me after fanning away my pipe smoke.

"Yes, let's see how Fisnik's getting on."

"I should be able to have a little ride on him soon. You too, if you want."

"I'll just film you, love, when he's got all his strength back."

Fisnik was a donkey that we'd sponsored, you see, and it was a pleasure to watch him filling out and looking more and more cheerful as the weeks went by.

# Epilogue

After writing that last sentence I put the top back on my pen and handed my notebooks to Doreen.

"That's my book finished. I'm off out for a stroll."

"Hmm, there are a lot of crossings out," she said, reaching for her reading specs.

"That's because I'm a perfectionist."

"If you're such a perfectionist, you can write it out again neatly."

"Ha! What for? Didn't you once call writing cath-something?"

"Cathartic."

"That's the word. Well, that's quite enough cathartics for me for a while. See you in a bit."

When I got back from my stroll, plus a few beers with Fede in the bar, it was quite late, and I found Doreen dozing with one of my notebooks in her lap.

"I'm back, dear."

"Hmm, ah, there you are. You know, Ken, this isn't as bad as I thought it would be." She patted the notebook.

"Ah."

"I think I'll type it out on the computer."

"Rather you than me."

"And tidy it up a bit."

"Feel free."

"It still needs an ending though," she said, peering at me over her specs like the prim librarian who used to tell me off at the last library I went to, fifty-odd years ago.

"What else is there to tell?"

"Well, about our trip to England, for one thing."

"Pah! I write for fun, not to make myself miserable," I said, shuddering at the thought of that damp, depressing fortnight in August spent mostly at my mother's house.

"You should compare and contrast your time back there with your new life here," she said.

"That's easy." I chucked her a pen. "Write this: Spain is great and England is still as rubbish as ever. The end."

"That would just spoil that nice bit about our donkey. You need to wind things up. You know, tell the readers that we're still renting our house out to that nice family, and things like that."

"They're a nice family now, are they? So you've got over your lesbophobia then, if that's a word."

"It is," said the frequenter of the writing group who wrote about a page a week. "It was just a bit of a shock that first time when I saw they were two ladies."

"I told you they'd be great tenants."

"Yes, the house was spotless and they're ever so nice, the kids too. Anyway, if you don't finish this off, I'm not typing it up," she said, handing me the notebook.

"Hmm, I'll finish it off then, but in my own way. It's about time *you* wrote something, anyway."

"I know, but the more you talk about writing, the harder it seems."

"Just write. After you've typed out mine, that is."

I nipped into my den, wrote the above, and that, as they say, is that.

# The End

doreenbtonks@gmail.com

Printed in Great Britain
by Amazon